T0183696

# Lecture Notes in Computer Science 11332

Commenced Publication in 1973
Founding and Former Series Editors:
Gerhard Goos, Juris Hartmanis, and Jan van Leeuwen

## Editorial Board

More information about this series at http://www.springer.com/series/7407

Dalibor Klusáček · Walfredo Cirne
Narayan Desai (Eds.)

# Job Scheduling Strategies for Parallel Processing

22nd International Workshop, JSSPP 2018
Vancouver, BC, Canada, May 25, 2018
Revised Selected Papers

 Springer

*Editors*
Dalibor Klusáček
CESNET
Prague, Czech Republic

Narayan Desai
Google
Seattle, WA, USA

Walfredo Cirne
Google
Mountain View, CA, USA

ISSN 0302-9743            ISSN 1611-3349   (electronic)
Lecture Notes in Computer Science
ISBN 978-3-030-10631-7         ISBN 978-3-030-10632-4   (eBook)
https://doi.org/10.1007/978-3-030-10632-4

Library of Congress Control Number: 2018965504

LNCS Sublibrary: SL1 – Theoretical Computer Science and General Issues

This Springer imprint is published by the registered company Springer Nature Switzerland AG
The registered company address is: Gewerbestrasse 11, 6330 Cham, Switzerland

# Preface

This volume contains the papers presented at the 22nd workshop on Job Scheduling Strategies for Parallel Processing that was held in Vancouver, Canada, on May 25, 2018, in conjunction with the 32nd IEEE International Parallel and Distributed Processing Symposium (IPDPS 2018). The proceedings of previous workshops are also available from Springer as LNCS volumes 949, 1162, 1291, 1459, 1659, 1911, 2221, 2537, 2862, 3277, 3834, 4376, 4942, 5798, 6253, 7698, 8429, 8828, 10353, and 10773.

This year 12 papers were submitted to the workshop, of which we accepted seven. All submitted papers went through a complete review process, with the full version being read and evaluated by an average of four reviewers. We would like to especially thank to our Program Committee members and additional reviewers for their willingness to participate in this effort and their excellent, detailed, thoughtful reviews.

From its very beginning, JSSPP has strived to balance practice and theory in its program while encouraging vivid discussions with the audience. This combination was repeatedly shown to provide a rich environment for technical debate about scheduling approaches. This year, the workshop opened with a keynote delivered by John Wilkes. Principal Engineer at Google, John motivated and described Google's *Flex*, the key piece of Google's resource management system. The main goal of *Flex* is to assure that internal users have access to enough resources to meet their business needs. Doing it efficiently, reliably, and scalably (i.e., with little human intervention) is very challenging. John described how techniques like controlled over-subscription, risk management, and leveraging different service-level objectives are used to meet this challenge. The presentation is available at: http://jsspp.org/papers18/Google-Flex-JSSPP.pdf.

Papers accepted for this year's JSSPP focused on several interesting problems in resource management and scheduling domain. The first two papers discuss the issues related to imprecise job walltimes estimates. Job walltimes estimates, usually specified by users, are known to be very imprecise, which causes problems both to the users and to the scheduling policies. Soysal et al. present a novel approach to use job metadata for job classification and improved walltime prediction. Klusáček et al. present an experimental analysis that discusses how the use of walltime predictors impacts the actual performance of a job scheduler.

Azevedo and Suter present an experience report from a real infrastructure, describing their efforts to reduce the need for a "human expert" when scheduling large HTC workloads in a system that is subject to many operational constraints that may impede the optimization efforts of the scheduler.

Merzkyet et al. describe a new pilot-based scheduling system called RADICAL-Pilot. Unlike classic HPC scheduling systems that schedule jobs on a job-per-job basis, pilot-based systems decouple workload specification, resource selection, and task execution via job placeholders and late-binding, helping to satisfy the resource requirements of workloads comprising multiple tasks. In their paper,

Merzkyet et al. describe RADICAL-Pilot's design, architecture, and implementation, and characterize the good performance of RADICAL-Pilot when executing multiple concurrent tasks.

Bashizade et al. propose a dynamic mechanism for sharing GPUs among multiple tenants, i.e., users. This adaptive simultaneous multi-tenancy allows the GPU to be shared among multiple kernels, as opposed to single-kernel multi-tenancy that only runs one kernel on the GPU at any given time and static simultaneous multi-tenancy that does not adapt to events in the system. By dynamically adjusting the kernels' parameters at run-time — when a new kernel arrives or a running kernel ends — Bashizade et al. show that system throughput is improved by an average of 9.8%, compared with sequentially executed kernels.

Bhuiyan et al. present a stochastic optimization-based framework for robust decision-making in the selection of distributed resources for scientific workflows with uncertain demands over a given planning horizon. Using their novel two-stage stochastic programming model for resource selection, they demonstrate up to 30% and 54% cost reductions relative to solutions lacking explicit considerations of demand uncertainties for 24-month and 36-month planning horizons, respectively.

Last but not least, Abdelmoamen et al. present an approach to control resource usage among multiple tenants in a distributed system. In their approach they built upon the concept of actors, which are autonomous concurrently executing active objects. In this paper, authors compare two different ways of supporting resource control for actor systems built using the Scala's Akka library. Abdelmoamen et al. then experimentally establish the performance cost of using these approaches, as well as their impact on resource utilization.

We hope you can join us at the next JSSPP workshop, this time in Rio de Janeiro, Brazil, on May 24, 2019. Enjoy your reading!

September 2018                                                    Walfredo Cirne
                                                                 Narayan Desai
                                                                 Dalibor Klusáček

# Organization

## Workshop Organizers

Walfredo Cirne       Google, USA
Narayan Desai       Google, USA
Dalibor Klusáček       CESNET, Czech Republic

## Program Committee

| | |
|---|---|
| Henri Casanova | University of Hawaii at Manoa, USA |
| Julita Corbalan | Barcelona Supercomputing Center, Spain |
| Hyeonsang Eom | Seoul National University, South Korea |
| Dror Feitelson | Hebrew University, Israel |
| Liana Fong | IBM T. J. Watson Research Center, USA |
| Eitan Frachtenberg | Facebook, USA |
| Alfredo Goldman | University of Sao Paulo, USA |
| Allan Gottlieb | New York University, USA |
| Virajith Jalaparti | Microsoft, USA |
| Kostantinos Karanasos | Microsoft, USA |
| Zhiling Lan | Illinois Institute of Technology, USA |
| Bill Nitzberg | Altair, USA |
| P-O. Östberg | Umeå University, Sweden |
| Larry Rudolph | Two Sigma, USA |
| Gonzalo Rodrigo | Berkeley Lab, USA |
| Uwe Schwiegelshohn | TU Dortmund University, Germany |
| Yingchong Situ | Google, USA |
| Leonel Sousa | Universidade de Lisboa, Portugal |
| Mark Squillante | IBM, USA |
| Wei Tang | Google, USA |
| Ramin Yahyapour | University of Göttingen, Germany |

## Additional Reviewers

Emilio Francesquini
Pedro Bruel
Sergio Santander-Jiménez

# Contents

# Analysis of Job Metadata for Enhanced Wall Time Prediction

Mehmet Soysal$^{(\boxtimes)}$, Marco Berghoff, and Achim Streit

Steinbuch Centre for Computing (SCC), Karlsruhe Institute of Technology (KIT),
Hermann-von-Helmholtz-Platz 1, 76344 Eggenstein-Leopoldshafen, Germany
{mehmet.soysal,marco.berghoff,achim.streit}@kit.edu

**Abstract.** For efficient utilization of large-scale HPC systems, the task of resource management and job scheduling is of highest priority. Therefore, modern job scheduling systems require information about the estimated total wall time of the jobs already at submission time. Proper wall time estimates are a key for reliable scheduling decisions. Typically, users specify these estimates, already at submission time, based on either previous knowledge or certain limits given by the system. Real-world experience shows that user given estimates are far away from accurate. Hence, an automated system is desirable that creates more precise wall time estimates of submitted jobs. In this paper, we investigate different job metadata and their impact on the wall time prediction. For the job wall time prediction, we used machine learning methods and the workload traces of large HPC systems. In contrast to previous work, we also consider the jobname and in particular the submission directory. Our evaluation shows that we can better predict the accuracy of jobs per user by a factor of seven than most users, without any in-depth analysis of the job.

## 1 Introduction

For the execution of applications on HPC systems, a so-called job is created and submitted to a queue. A job describes the application, needed resources, and requested wall time. An HPC scheduler manages the queue and orders the jobs for efficient use of the resources. The jobs are waiting in the queue until the requested resources are available. The scheduler allocates the resources and starts the job [1]. For planning future usage of the resources, schedulers typically use a wall time that corresponds to the maximum execution time for each job. This wall time, also known as estimated job runtime or wall clock time, is usually given by the user, or a default value of the system is applied.

Often, users could be able to do a reasonable job runtime estimation, because they have detailed knowledge about their jobs. Nevertheless, the users tend to request more time then the job needs, to prevent jobs being terminated too early by the scheduler. This detailed knowledge is not available without interviewing the user. Without this knowledge, it is difficult for the scheduler to perform exact resource planning. Without accurate job wall time estimation, it is almost

© Springer Nature Switzerland AG 2019
D. Klusáček et al. (Eds.): JSSPP 2018, LNCS 11332, pp. 1–14, 2019.
https://doi.org/10.1007/978-3-030-10632-4_1

impossible to make any preparation of the system for future job requirements. This challenge is more important if the HPC systems become larger. For future exascale systems, this can help to improve the overall efficiency significantly. The project ADA-FS [2] (as part of the DFG-funded priority program 1648 "Software for Exascale Computing" SPPEXA) focuses on pre-staging of input data for massively parallel jobs. Previous to the data staging it is going to deploy a private filesystem across the allocated nodes. For this, it is essential to know on which nodes a queued job will be executed. The scheduler predicts these nodes based on the user given wall times of the already running jobs. Hence, precise wall time estimates are critical.

In this paper, we take a closer look at the individual metadata and examine their impact on the prediction. Machine learning methods are used to determine the influence of additional metadata. In particular, we use previously unconsidered metadata for jobs in the workload traces of our HPC systems to support the machine learning methods, e.g., information about the working directory of jobs, which typically contains valuable information about the jobs itself.

The remainder of this paper is structured as follows: In Sect. 2 we give a brief introduction to machine learning and similar approaches. We show in Sect. 3 how we prepared our historical data and also explain metrics to rate our results. In Sect. 4 we present the results on the used metadata and finish with a conclusion and outlook to future work in Sect. 5.

## 2   Related Work

### 2.1   Predicting Job Walltimes

Enhanced predictions of HPC job wall time can be used to improve the scheduling performance [3]. With exact information about the runtime of a job, the scheduler can predict more accurately when sufficient resources are available to start queued jobs. [4]. However, the user requested wall time is not close to the real used wall time. Gibbons [3,5], and Downey [4] use historical workloads to predict the wall times of parallel applications. They predict wall times based on templates. These templates are created by analyzing previously collected metadata and grouped according to similarities. However, both approaches are restricted to simple definitions. Smith et al. [6,7] applied greedy and genetic search techniques to identify similar jobs and partition them into categories. The studies as mentioned above use templates to find similarities and use these for wall time predictions. In our evaluation, we do not use templates. In the recent years, the machine learning algorithms are used to predict resource consumption in several studies [5,8–13]. However, these studies do not take into account the additional metadata we do. There is also a online prediction system available for the XSEDE [14] resources – KARNAK [15]. Karnak also uses machine learning to provide a prediction for users either when their job will start, or how long a hypothetical job would wait before starting on selected XSEDE resources. For this prediction the requested wall time, processors, queue, and the system has to be provided. In our evaluation we consider more metadata.

## 2.2   Machine Learning

Machine learning (ML) is about knowledge retrieval from data. It can also be understood as statistical learning and predictive analytics. In general, machine learning is a method to learn from a set of samples with a target value and use the learned data to predict target values from unknown samples. For our evaluation, we use a supervised machine learning approach [16].

In supervised learning, an algorithm is used to train a model with input data and its associated output. This process is called training. A trained model predicts the desired output value from new input samples. However, the success of the method relies on expert knowledge in the machine learning discipline, to pre-process the input data and to select the correct model including the optimization of parameters. These tasks are very complicated and time-consuming. Therefore, there is a high demand for automatizing the machine learning process, so the use of *Automatic Machine Learning (AUTOML)* has gained high acceptance in a variety of domains. In our evaluation, the AUTOML library auto-sklearn [17] (based on scikit-learn [18,19]) is used to automate the complex work of machine learning optimization. In a classical ML process, different models and systems are explored until the best is chosen. Auto-sklearn estimates the best performing model out of a range of various classifiers or pre-processors. The training of the model can be time and resource consuming until an accurate model is found. Therefore, the training can be time-limited.

## 3   Methods

For the prediction of the wall times, machine learning models are trained with historical workload data. A large collection of parallel workload traces is available online [20]. The Parallel Workloads Archive offers workload traces in the standard workload format [21]. Our workload traces enhances this standard workload format. For example, it also offers the initial working directory (IWD) or the jobname. Here, we have to note that these metadata fields may contain privacy-sensitive information which should not be published online.

For our evaluation, we use the recorded workloads from two of the HPC-systems at the Karlsruhe Institute for Technology, the ForHLR I + II [22,23]. These workload traces are generated for the accounting system to track resource consumption. The reason for the job termination is not recorded in these logs, e.g., for technical reasons, by the user, or by the scheduler. It should also be taken into account that there are similar problems with the parallel workload archives as described by Feitelson et al. [24].

Incorrect entries have been removed from our records. Also, jobs with shortly used wall time are eliminated, which indicates technical problems. 177 users remain for the ForHLR I cluster with a total of 169 358 jobs. 107 143 jobs from 135 users stay for the ForHLR II cluster for our evaluation. The used metadata entries from the traces are explained below.

## 3.1  Job Metadata

The *used walltime* describes the real runtime used by the job in seconds. Jobs with a used wall time less than 60 s are discarded, to ignore jobs with mistakes in the start script. The aim of our approach is to predict a value close to the used wall time, hence, this is the target value for the AUTOML model.

Like mentioned earlier, the human given *requested walltimes* are anything but ideal. The requested wall time is considered because users might use smaller wall times for short test runs and longer wall times for the simulation. The maximum wall time on both machines is three days. The users can omit to specify the requested wall time, then the default value of 10 min is automatically applied. The requested wall time is an integer representing the required time in seconds.

*Queues* are associated with each job. Usually, the system operators define available resources for the specific queues, e.g., higher priority or specialized hardware. Both clusters offer a "develop" queue with higher priority but reduced maximum wall time. The queue name is converted into a categorical value to make it usable for machine learning.

The requested *taskcount*—the number of requested cores— is a user requested value. Some users tend to use a small task count to test their simulations before they run the real workload. Like wall time, the task count is used as an integer value. For example, Fig. 1 shows a subset of categorized datasets from two users based on the requested wall time and task count. User A with 249 jobs used two different task counts. The used wall time of the jobs are within a small range and can be easily predicted. User B has submitted 214 jobs, all with identical task count. Here, the used wall time is spread over a large range. This shows that the given input values (requested wall time and task count) are not sufficient to predict the job wall time for user B.

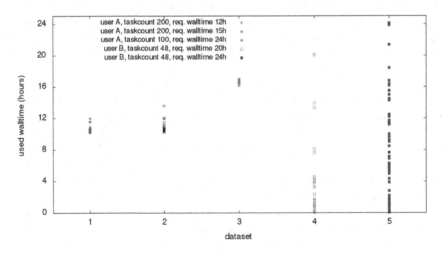

**Fig. 1.** Categorized dataset for two users, based on the requested walltime and taskcount.

*SubmitTime* represents the time of job submission, *StartTime* the time when the job starts to execute. The users usually observe jobs submitted during business hours. Submitting jobs right before the weekend result in unobserved runs. If users see unplanned behavior in their job, they will cancel them and restart. While this behavior is very user specific, jobs submitted and started at the the weekend will likely run until the simulation finishes or the requested wall time ends and the job gets canceled by the scheduler. To take this observation into account, the day of the week and the hour of the day was sampled from the SubmitTime and StartTime (Table 1).

**Table 1.** Example creation of the input matrix for two jobnames.

| jobname | myjob | jan | feb | 10 | 16 | 18 |
|---|---|---|---|---|---|---|
| myjob_jan.16-18 | 1 | 1 | 0 | 0 | 1 | 1 |
| myjob_feb.10-18 | 1 | 0 | 1 | 1 | 0 | 1 |

At least two job parameters are a free chosen string by the user, the *jobname* and the *initial working directory (IWD)*. While some users set a specific jobname for each job, others do not use a jobname at all. There are also some users, which use a specific jobname for specific parts of a work, e.g., preprocessing, simulation, and post-processing. More interestingly, in real-world, it can often be observed, that users organize their jobs by either jobname or the IWD. We split both parameters into smaller components to gather additional information. For the jobname, we use a generic regular expression to split the string by the following delimiter "_|-| |.". The split string is then converted to a matrix. For splitting the IWD a regular expression is used to separate the directory path into three components. The first part points to the parallel file systems. This separates jobs using the regular home file system or the optimized and faster scratch file system. The second and third parts contain the directory, where the third part is the basename of the working directory. Table 2 shows a small example, how directories are converted into a matrix for the machine learning.

**Table 2.** Example creation of the input matrix for directory names.

| IWD | /p1/joe-abc | /p3/joe-xyz | sim | data | run_a | data/run | x_1 | x_2 | x_3 |
|---|---|---|---|---|---|---|---|---|---|
| /p1/joe-abc/sim/run_a | 1 | 0 | 1 | 0 | 1 | 0 | 0 | 0 | 0 |
| /p3/joe-xyz/data/run_a | 0 | 1 | 0 | 1 | 1 | 0 | 0 | 0 | 0 |
| /p1/joe-abc/data/run/x_1 | 1 | 0 | 0 | 0 | 0 | 1 | 1 | 0 | 0 |
| /p1/joe-abc/data/run/x_2 | 1 | 0 | 0 | 0 | 0 | 1 | 0 | 1 | 0 |
| /p1/joe-abc/data/run/x_3 | 1 | 0 | 0 | 0 | 0 | 1 | 0 | 0 | 1 |

## 3.2   Metrics

The built-in metrics from the scikit library [25] are used to evaluate the trained models. Scikit offers several metrics for the regression tasks. The $R^2$ score (coefficient of determination) provides a metric how well the trained model will predict new samples. It is defined by

$$R^2(y, \hat{y}) = 1 - \frac{\sum_{i=0}^{n_{\text{samples}}-1} (y_i - \hat{y}_i)^2}{\sum_{i=0}^{n_{\text{samples}}-1} (y_i - \bar{y})^2},$$

(1)

where $y_i$ is the real used walltime and $\hat{y}_i$ is the predicted value of the $i$-th sample, and

$$\bar{y} = \frac{1}{n_{\text{samples}}} \sum_{i=0}^{n_{\text{samples}}-1} y_i,$$

(2)

where $\bar{y}$ as the average of $y_i$. The best possible value is 1.0 which corresponds to a perfect prediction. The $R^2$ score can also be negative and indicates a badly trained model [26]. Other metrics are the mean absolute error (MAE) [27] and the median absolute error (MedAE) [28]. Both measure the difference between predicted and used wall time. MAE is the mean over all pairs of predicted and used wall time,

$$\text{MAE}(y, \hat{y}) = \frac{1}{n_{\text{samples}}} \sum_{i=0}^{n_{\text{samples}}-1} |y_i - \hat{y}_i|.$$

(3)

MedAE is the median value of these pairs,

$$\text{MedAE}(y, \hat{y}) = \text{median}(|y_1 - \hat{y}_1|, \dots, |y_n - \hat{y}_n|).$$

(4)

In contrast to MAE, MedAE is robust against outliers. The individual users' historical workload traces are divided into two parts. For this purpose, scikit-learn provides a function that divides the data into a test dataset and a training dataset. The default value is to use 25% as test data and the remaining as training data. A random selection decides which records are added to which set [29]. The training dataset is used to train the machine model, called training set. A high $R^2$ score for the training data implies that AUTOML was able to find a good model. The other part is used to test the trained model, called test set. A high $R^2$ score on the test set indicates that the trained model makes good predictions. In our case, this means that the predicted wall time of the job is close to the used wall time. Figure 2 shows the results of AUTOML trained with all above mentioned metadata: requested wall time, task count, initial working dir, jobname, class, start time, and submit time. Each point represents a pair of the $R^2$ scores from the training and test set for a specific user of the machines (ForHLR I+II). In Fig. 2 an accumulation of the pairs in the right upper half can be seen, which indicate that a well-trained model for most of the users are found. Some low scores for the ForHLR II users indicates, that better model for ForHLR I users are found.

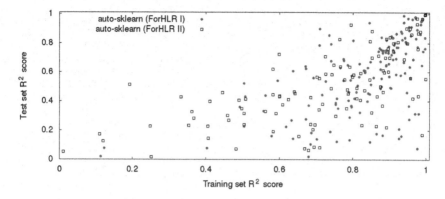

**Fig. 2.** $X$-Axis $R^2$ score on training samples, $Y$-Axis $R^2$ score on test samples for ForHLR I+II with 20 min auto-sklearn.

## 4  Results

The AUTOML model predicted wall times are compared to the user requested wall times. Therefore, a separate model for each user is trained, and then the $R^2$ score for the prediction calculated. Figure 3 shows a cumulative distribution plot of the accuracies for the models for the different users for the ForHLR I. For the training of the AUTOML model, we used a training set with the requested walltime as metadata. Besides, we extend the requested wall time with other metadata records, e.g., req. wall time + task count, req. wall time + jobname, req. wall time + start time, and so on. Finally, all available metadata are used to train the AUTOML model. Ideally, a curve should be flat at the beginning and rise late (high $R^2$ prediction scores). In contrast, 80 % of users have a negative $R^2$ score based on user estimated wall times on ForHLR I. In Fig. 5a and b these results are grouped into four categories of the $R^2$ scores for the ForHLR I+II. The ranges less 0 and from 0 to 0.5 show a really bad and bad trained model. Whereas in the two ranges from 0.5 to 0.8 and 0.8 to 1 indicate a good and excellent trained model. The four fields have been selected to illustrate the improvement in the individual areas. Adding the different fields of the metadata the number of user in the low $R^2$ ranges decreases and increases in the high ranges. A model trained with all metadata shows the best results. Similar results for ForHLR II are plotted in Figs. 4 and 5b. Based on user estimated walltimes on ForHLR II over 90 % of the users have a negative $R^2$ score. In the Table 3 we used the metric MAE (mean absolute error) to present the results based on time. For this purpose, we have grouped the users according to the wall time accuracy. The last line shows the MAE value of the user's requested wall time as the prediction and compares it to the used wall time of the jobs. While only eight users have a mean absolute error less than 30 min, over 127 users are more than 6 h mean absolute error with their requested wall time. While AUTOML achieves even with a few metadata fields good results.

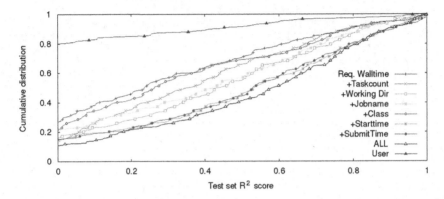

**Fig. 3.** $X$-axis $R^2$ score on test samples, $Y$-axis cumulative distribution for ForHLR I.

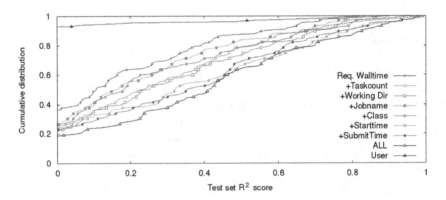

**Fig. 4.** $X$-axis $R^2$ score on test samples, $Y$-axis cumulative distribution for ForHLR II.

**Table 3.** Number of users categorized in mean absolute error (MAE) values for the ForHLR I+II.

| | ForHLR I | | | | ForHLR II | | | |
|---|---|---|---|---|---|---|---|---|
| Req. Walltime | 30min | 30min-3h | 3h-6h | 6h- | 30min-3h | 30min-3h | 3h-6h | 6h- |
| +req. Walltime | 22 | 42 | 29 | 84 | 28 | 40 | 25 | 42 |
| +IWD | 28 | 44 | 34 | 71 | 32 | 47 | 14 | 42 |
| +StartTime | 29 | 49 | 41 | 58 | 30 | 45 | 25 | 35 |
| +SubmitTime | 32 | 47 | 43 | 55 | 31 | 42 | 25 | 37 |
| +TaskCount | 28 | 39 | 29 | 81 | 32 | 42 | 18 | 43 |
| +Jobname | 24 | 45 | 33 | 75 | 30 | 40 | 21 | 44 |
| +Class | 26 | 41 | 32 | 78 | 32 | 39 | 19 | 45 |
| ALL | 31 | 52 | 42 | 52 | 33 | 46 | 21 | 35 |
| User | 8 | 22 | 20 | 127 | 10 | 21 | 21 | 83 |

It is noticeable that on both machines the start time and submit time make a significant contribution to accuracy. In Figs. 6 and 7 we show the results using the date components of submittime and starttime. For this, we used the requested wall time together with the hour of day component (Fig. 6) of the start time and submit time. The day of the week component is presented in Fig. 7. The third line show the results of all job metadata (requested walltime, taskcount, initial working dir, jobname, class, starttime, and submittime), while using only the date components for submittime and starttime.

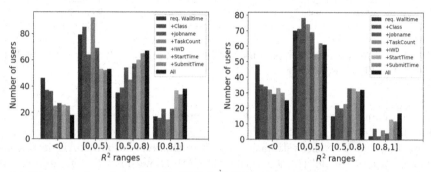

(a) $Y$-axis number of users for ForHLR I   (b) $Y$-axis number of users for ForHLR II.

**Fig. 5.** Histogram of categories of the $R^2$ score

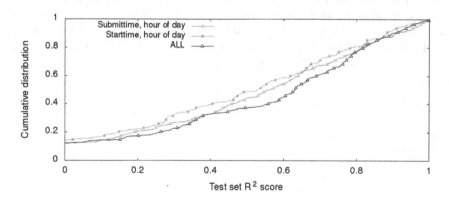

**Fig. 6.** $X$-axis $R^2$ score on test samples, $Y$-axis cumulative distribution for ForHLR I with only StartTime hour.

All three lines in both figures are very close together, which indicates that the components, hour of day and day of week, from StartTime and SubmitTime provide significant information for the model.

In Figs. 8 and 9 the comparison of the user prediction and AUTOML trained models can be seen. Figure 8 the mean aboslute error (MAE) in hours. Figure 9

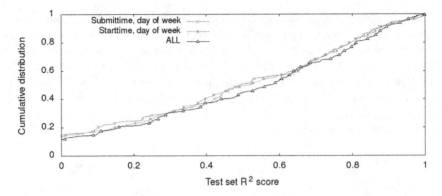

**Fig. 7.** $X$-axis $R^2$ score on test samples, $Y$-axis cumulative distribution for ForHLR I with only StartTime weekday.

shows the cumulative distribution for the median absolute error (medAE) in hours and in both Figures the horizontal line at 0.6 on the $Y$-Axis represents 60 % of the users. The user estimations, of both clusters, has a medAE deviation of about 7.4 h. A model trained with AUTOML shows for 60 % of the users a medAE of approximately 1 h on the ForHLR I and 1.4 h for the FORHLR II. Figure 8 shows the difference for 60 % of the users using MAE as a metric. Using AUTOML improves the accuracy from 15.4 h (user estimation) to 4.6 h (AutoML). The accuracy of the predictions for the ForHLR II improve from almost 16 h to only 3 h by AUTOML. Taking into account that only job metadata is used without a knowledge of the payload, this is a good result. More detailed knowledge about the job could result in better predictions, but require in-depth knowledge about the tools and applications of the users. This can not be done in an automated way for the vast number of users.

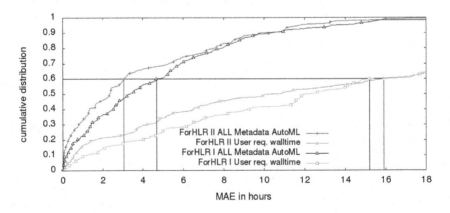

**Fig. 8.** Comparison of MAE for ForHLR I+II. X-axis mean absolute error in hours, Y-axis cumulative distribution.

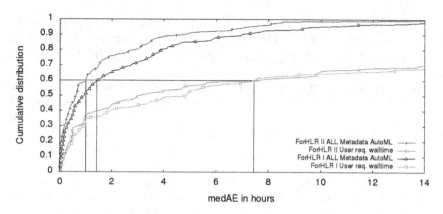

**Fig. 9.** Comparison of medAE for ForHLR I+II. X-axis Median absolute error in hours, Y-Axis cumulative distribution.

A trained model can be saved to disk for model persistence. This file can be then loaded within seconds and subsequently be used for further predictions [30].

The size of the compressed trained model files are up to 280 MB per user on the ForHLR I and 214 MB on the ForHLR II. The average size is around 23 MB per user. We use a generic regular expression of the job name and the working directory, without any further processing. This leads to a drastic increase in the dimension of the input data. For top users, this results in up to 5000 columns for input parameters. These high numbers are caused by the user giving his directories and jobs names which contain many characters of our regular expression. Analyzing this high dimension can cause the well-known problem "curse of dimensionality" [31,32]. The problem describes issues with high dimensional data. Data with increasing dimension becomes sparse. This sparsity is problematic for any machine learning methods. In our case, a user creating a new directory for every job could make the information of the working directory useless for us, because no more correlations can be recognized as each date is individual. AUTOML use a principal component analysis [33] to reduce the dimension of the input parameter by omitting meaningless columns. This helps to reduce this issue, but this process needs more time and resources to recognize meaningless dimensions. Another approach could be to apply a compression algorithm on these user chosen strings or to discard meaningless names right before training the machine model.

## 5   Conclusion and Future Work

In this work, we have shown that all the chosen job metadata contains information which improves the wall time predictions. In particular, the previously unnoticed metadata for the initial working directory and jobname provide an additional source of information. Automatic prediction of job wall times is possible without an in-depth analysis of user data and behavior. Good prediction models can be trained with very simple job metadata without having precise knowledge of the user's work. The expressiveness of the job metadata depends on the operating model of each supercomputer and the way the users use that machine.

A further examination with workload traces from other machines will be conducted in the future, e.g., from other HPC systems in Germany, as our approach uses general job metadata as long as enough metadata like the jobname and initial working directory is available. These are available in most schedulers. The preprocessing of the data is also generic so that no cluster-specific parameters are used.

Providing these predictions to the scheduler is the next step. This means that the scheduler can use the prediction as a basis for its planning; instead, the user requested wall time. The user requested wall time could be used as a guaranteed wall time and the planning could be done with the predicted wall time.

Another necessary investigation is the accuracy of predictions over time. A model that has been trained could become inaccurate over time due to a change of the user behavior, i.e., submitting different workloads and applications in the jobs. Another topic is the fundamental problem with unknown users, known as the cold start. In our approach, a model is trained for each user. There is no model for new users which we can use for prediction. A possible solution for the cold start problem could be an evaluation with a model containing all the job records of all users.

**Acknowledgement.** This work inside of the project ADA-FS is funded by the DFG Priority Program "Software for Exascale Computing" (SPPEXA, SPP 1648), which is gratefully acknowledged.

# References

1. Hovestadt, M., Kao, O., Keller, A., Streit, A.: Scheduling in HPC resource management systems: queuing vs. planning. In: Feitelson, D., Rudolph, L., Schwiegelshohn, U. (eds.) JSSPP 2003. LNCS, vol. 2862, pp. 1–20. Springer, Heidelberg (2003). https://doi.org/10.1007/10968987_1
2. Oeste, S., Kluge, M., Soysal, M., Streit, A., Vef, M., Brinkmann, A.: Exploring opportunities for job-temporal file systems with ada-fs. In: 1st Joint International Workshop on Parallel Data Storage and Data Intensive Scalable Computing Systems (2016)
3. Gibbons, R.: A historical application profiler for use by parallel schedulers. In: Feitelson, D.G., Rudolph, L. (eds.) JSSPP 1997. LNCS, vol. 1291, pp. 58–77. Springer, Heidelberg (1997). https://doi.org/10.1007/3-540-63574-2_16
4. Downey, A.B.: Predicting queue times on space-sharing parallel computers. In: 11th International Proceedings on Parallel Processing Symposium, pp. 209–218. IEEE (1997)
5. Gibbons, R.: A historical profiler for use by parallel schedulers. Master's thesis, University of Toronto (1997)
6. Smith, W., Foster, I., Taylor, V.: Predicting application run times using historical information. In: Feitelson, D.G., Rudolph, L. (eds.) JSSPP 1998. LNCS, vol. 1459, pp. 122–142. Springer, Heidelberg (1998). https://doi.org/10.1007/BFb0053984

7. Smith, W., Taylor, V., Foster, I.: Using run-time predictions to estimate queue wait times and improve scheduler performance. In: Feitelson, D.G., Rudolph, L. (eds.) JSSPP 1999. LNCS, vol. 1659, pp. 202–219. Springer, Heidelberg (1999). https://doi.org/10.1007/3-540-47954-6_11

8. Matsunaga, A., AB Fortes, J.: On the use of machine learning to predict the time and resources consumed by applications. In: Proceedings of the 2010 10th IEEE/ACM International Conference on Cluster, Cloud and Grid Computing, pp. 495–504. IEEE Computer Society (2010)

9. Kapadia, N.H., AB Fortes, J.: On the design of a demand-based network-computing system: the purdue university network-computing hubs. In: Proceedings of the Seventh International Symposium on High Performance Distributed Computing, pp. 71–80. IEEE (1998)

10. Mu'alem, A.W., Feitelson, D.G.: Utilization, predictability, workloads, and user runtime estimates in scheduling the ibm sp2 with backfilling. IEEE Trans. Parallel Distrib. Syst. 12(6), 529–543 (2001)

11. Nadeem, F., Fahringer, T.: Using templates to predict execution time of scientific workflow applications in the grid. In: Proceedings of the 2009 9th IEEE/ACM International Symposium on Cluster Computing and the Grid, pp. 316–323. IEEE Computer Society (2009)

12. Smith, W.: Prediction services for distributed computing. In: IEEE International Parallel and Distributed Processing Symposium, IPDPS 2007, pp. 1–10. IEEE (2007)

13. Tsafrir, D., Etsion, Y., Feitelson, D.G.: Backfilling using system-generated predictions rather than user runtime estimates. IEEE Trans. Parallel Distrib. Syst. 18(6), 789–803 (2007)

14. Xsede. https://www.xsede.org/

15. Karnak start/wait time predictions. http://karnak.xsede.org/karnak/index.html

16. Mohri, M., Rostamizadeh, A., Talwalkar, A.: Foundations of Machine Learning. MIT Press, Cambridge (2012)

17. Feurer, M., Klein, A., Eggensperger, K., Springenberg, J., Blum, M., Hutter, F.: Efficient and robust automated machine learning. In: Cortes, C., Lawrence, N.D., Lee, D.D., Sugiyama, M., Garnett, R. (eds.) Advances in Neural Information Processing Systems, vol. 28, pp. 2962–2970. Curran Associates Inc., New York (2015)

18. Pedregosa, F., et al.: Scikit-learn: machine learning in Python. J. Mach. Learn. Res. 12, 2825–2830 (2011)

19. Buitinck, L., et al.: API design for machine learning software: experiences from the scikit-learn project. In: ECML PKDD Workshop: Languages for Data Mining and Machine Learning, pp. 108–122 (2013)

20. Parallel Workloads Archive. http://www.cs.huji.ac.il/labs/parallel/workload/

21. The Standard Workload Format. http://www.cs.huji.ac.il/labs/parallel/workload/swf.html

22. Forhlr i, kit/scc. https://www.scc.kit.edu/dienste/forhlr1.php

23. Forhlr ii, kit/scc. https://www.scc.kit.edu/dienste/forhlr2.php

24. Feitelson, D.G., Tsafrir, D., Krakov, D.: Experience with using the parallel workloads archive. J. Parallel Distrib. Comput. 74(10), 2967–2982 (2014)

25. scikit - regression metrics. http://scikit-learn.org/stable/modules/model_evaluation.html#regression-metrics

26. scikit - r2 score. http://scikit-learn.org/stable/modules/generated/sklearn.metrics.r2_score.html#sklearn.metrics.r2_score

27. scikit - mean absolute error. http://scikit-learn.org/stable/modules/generated/sklearn.metrics.mean_absolute_error.html#sklearn.metrics.mean_absolute_error

28. scikit - median absolute error. http://scikit-learn.org/stable/modules/generated/sklearn.metrics.median_absolute_error.html#sklearn.metrics.median_absolute_error

29. scikit - datasset spliting

30. scikit - model persistence. http://scikit-learn.org/stable/modules/model_persistence.html

31. Bellman, R.: Dynamic Programming. Courier Corporation, North Chelmsford (2013)

32. Hughes, G.: On the mean accuracy of statistical pattern recognizers. IEEE Trans. Inf. Theory 14(1), 55–63 (1968)

33. Pearson, K.: LIII. on lines and planes of closest fit to systems of points in space. Lond, Edinb, Dublin Philos. Mag. J. Sci. 2(11), 559–572 (1901)

# Evaluating the Impact of Soft Walltimes on Job Scheduling Performance

Dalibor Klusáček$^{(\boxtimes)}$ and Václav Chlumský

CESNET a.l.e., Brno, Czech Republic
{klusacek,vchlumsky}@cesnet.cz

**Abstract.** For two decades researchers have been analyzing the impact of inaccurate job walltime (runtime) estimates on the performance of job scheduling algorithms, especially in case of backfilling. Several studies analyzed the pros and cons of using accurate vs. inaccurate estimates. Some researchers focused on the ways users of the system can be motivated to provide more accurate runtime estimates. The recent addition of so-called "soft walltime" parameter in the widely used PBS Professional enables a system administrator to actually use some of these techniques to refine user-provided walltime estimates. The obvious question of a system administrator is whether such walltime predictions are useful and "safe" and what will be the impact on the overall system performance. In this work, we use several detailed simulations to analyze the actual impact of using soft walltimes in a job scheduler, discussing the scenarios when such "refined" estimates can be meaningfully used.

**Keywords:** Job · Scheduling · Backfilling · Walltime estimate
Soft walltime

## 1 Introduction

In 1995, the seminal EASY backfilling [23] algorithm has been introduced and soon became defacto standard scheduling algorithm in all mainstream resource managers. Since then, many variants of the baseline backfilling have been proposed, e.g., backfilling with multiple job reservations [20], slack-based backfilling supporting priorities and bounded wait times [27] or conservative backfilling where each waiting job gets a reservation [18]. All variants of backfilling that use job reservation(s) have one thing in common. They rely on (inaccurate) job walltime estimates when (A) establishing job reservation(s), i.e., when determining the earliest expected start time for a queued job, and (B) when selecting "filler" jobs that must not collide with these existing reservation(s).

### 1.1 Walltime Estimates

In practice, these walltime estimates are typically very inaccurate and overestimated [10,18]. Existing computing systems often use a user's walltime estimate

© Springer Nature Switzerland AG 2019
D. Klusáček et al. (Eds.): JSSPP 2018, LNCS 11332, pp. 15–38, 2019.
https://doi.org/10.1007/978-3-030-10632-4_2

as the upper bound of job's runtime and kill the job when it exceeds its estimated walltime. This causes the relatively high overestimation. Second, scheduling systems also frequently classify jobs according to some default runtime limits. For example, there can be different job queues with different maximum job runtime defaults. Frequently, these default runtime values are then used by many jobs. As a result, most jobs in the system use only few common estimates and therefore "look similar" to the backfilling algorithm.

Overestimation and limited walltime variability then impede the effectiveness of backfilling on many levels [29]. First, predicted start time(s) for waiting job(s) are very inaccurate, while available "holes" in the schedule appear to be too small for waiting jobs which decreases utilization and throughput. This well-known fact motivated several researchers to either develop some form of runtime prediction technique or find a significant incentive for individual users to improve the accuracy of their runtime requests [4,16]. Although these efforts were significant, they remained mostly "academic" and most systems still face these problems due to several contributing factors.

We believe that there are two main reasons for this unfortunate situation that are surprisingly simple. First, it is just unrealistic to expect that users will thoroughly analyze their walltime requirements, updating them with each new job submission. Therefore, it is up to the resource manager or system administrator to develop and apply some automated technique. However, for many years mainstream resource managers were not prepared to provide *safe ways how to refine walltime estimates* without killing a job when a refined (smaller) estimate is exceeded. Fortunately, this situation has changed in 2017, when the mainstream PBS Professional delivered the concept of so-called *soft walltime* [26].

## 1.2   Soft Walltimes in PBS Professional

Soft walltimes are designed to safely *refine* user-provided job walltime (runtime) estimates. When enabled, the scheduler does not use user-provided estimates but instead uses so-called soft walltimes for all scheduling operations. Most importantly, it uses them to create job reservation(s) and perform backfilling. Soft walltimes are safe from the point of view of the user, because jobs are not killed when their soft walltimes are exceeded. As usual, a job is only killed when it exceeds its original, user-provided estimate. An important security feature is that soft walltimes cannot be specified or modified by users. Only the manager (system administrator) is allowed to setup them, typically using the so-called *job hook* script. This guarantees that users cannot obtain unfair priority in backfilling by providing very low (unrealistic) soft walltimes. More details on soft walltimes can be found in the documentation [26].

## 1.3   Paper Contribution and Structure

The main contribution of this paper is an experimental analysis that uses simulation to demonstrate the effect of soft walltimes on the job scheduling performance. Our goal was not the development of "yet another runtime prediction technique". Instead, we use four very trivial walltime prediction techniques to define soft walltimes and then show that even with such trivial techniques *the performance of the system can improve significantly*. The demonstration uses eight publicly available workload traces with different job characteristics and different estimate accuracies, showing the impact on average job wait times and slow-downs. Importantly, we provide detailed wait time analysis using *performance heatmaps* that show performance improvement or deterioration with respect to different job sizes (i.e., job lengths and CPU requirements).

We believe that this new soft walltime functionality available in the open-source PBS Professional together with our promising results—that are however based on very simple prediction techniques—can motivate a new round of practically oriented research on backfilling and runtime prediction techniques.

This paper is organized as follows. Section 2 briefly discusses the related work. Prediction techniques that were used to calculate soft walltimes in this paper are presented in Sect. 3. Experimental setup and simulation results are presented in Sect. 4. We conclude the paper in Sect. 5 and present possible future research directions related to soft walltimes.

## 2 Related Works

Many works have addressed the problem of inaccurate runtime estimates and the impact they have on the performance of backfilling. For quite some time, it was believed that the inaccuracy has little [11] or even positive effect on the performance of backfilling [4,10]. However, Tsafrir [29] has demonstrated that accuracy is in fact favorable, similarly to the variability of estimates. The major problem in some of those older works was that they used unrealistic (deterministic/randomized) *F*-model [10] to synthetically generate (inaccurate) user runtime estimates. However, as pointed out by Tsafrir [29,30], estimates generated by *F*-model provide too much information to the scheduler and do not correspond to the typical coarse-grained nature of user-provided estimates.

At the same time, researchers have considered ways how to obtain better job runtime estimates. One way is to try to motivate users by incentives. Authors of [16] have shown that even when users are motivated to improve the accuracy of their estimates—with the assurance that their jobs will not be killed if the improved estimates are too short—the accuracy of their new estimates was, on average, only slightly better than their original estimates [16].

In such situation, it is not surprising that several automated techniques have been proposed to establish more precise estimates. These techniques can be divided into several categories according to the applied estimation technique. The technique proposed in [5] uses repeated executions of the job to establish the estimate while other solutions work on the basis of compile-time analysis [2,21] or using a historical information together with the statistical analysis [25] of previously executed jobs. Such approach has been applied in [24] where the authors use a template-based approach to categorize and then predict job execution times. This approach is based on the observation that similar applications are more likely to have similar runtimes than applications that have nothing in common. The similarity is based on several parameters such as the type of the job, the owner of the job, the requested number of CPUs, etc. According to this information the jobs are divided into categories and the runtime estimate is computed using historical data [24]. Such categorization according to similarity has been used by many researchers [15,28].

Often, predicted runtimes were used to address a closely related issue of estimating queue wait times [15,19,25]. For example, the mean queue delay predictions are derived by simulating the future behavior of the scheduler [25], or a uniform-log distribution is used to model the remaining lifetimes of jobs currently executing to predict when required machine(s) will become available and thus when the job waiting at the head of the queue will start [6]. Also, fully automatic methods for predicting bounds (with specific levels of certainty) on the amount of queue delay each individual job will experience have been developed [19]. Although these methods often use some form of job runtime prediction, they are out of the scope of this paper.

We kindly refer, e.g., to this survey [22] for more details concerning various runtime prediction techniques.

## 3    Runtime Prediction Techniques

In order to evaluate the suitability of soft walltimes we have used four different ways of computing such "refined" runtime estimate that we describe in this section. We did not use any of the aforementioned advanced techniques but used rather straightforward and easy-to-compute predictions.

Each technique is working on a per-user basis, i.e., a new runtime estimate for a given job of a user is computed using information about previous jobs of that user[1]. Our first and most trivial solution uses the actual runtime of the last completed user's job as the new soft walltime for the newly arrived user's job (see Formula 1). The second solution depicted by Formula 2 keeps track of all runtimes of all completed user's jobs and uses the average runtime as the new soft walltime. Although these techniques are truly easy to implement, they are not very accurate. For example, if a given user is simultaneously using two different types of calculations (represented by short and long jobs), then the first technique will often either overestimate or underestimate the runtime significantly while the latter (average) will produce estimates that lie between those actual runtimes, i.e., such estimates will be always either over or underestimated.

$$soft\_walltime(job_i) = runtime(job_{i-1}) \tag{1}$$

$$soft\_walltime(job_i) = \frac{1}{i-1} \sum_{k=1}^{i-1} runtime(job_k) \tag{2}$$

---

[1] In case that a given user has no completed jobs so far then such historic information is obviously missing, thus we use the user-provided estimate instead.

In order to address this issue, the third and fourth solutions are somehow more complicated and do not use the actual job runtime directly. Instead, they measure the fraction of job's actual runtime and user's estimate (see $walltime_{usage}$ in Formula 3), i.e., they measure to what extent the estimated walltime was actually used. Since the user's estimate is the upper bound of job runtime[2], $walltime_{usage}$ falls between 0.0 and 1.0 representing the relative usage of requested walltime. In other words, the technique measures by how much a user overestimates job's runtime. It is fair to mention, that similar approach has been used in [28]. Once the $walltime_{usage}$ is computed, it is used by our third and fourth prediction techniques to generate a soft walltime.

The third prediction technique first computes the average of $walltime_{usage}$ values, i.e., it computes the fractions of used walltimes of all previously completed jobs, and then multiplies the walltime estimate of a new job by the average of these numbers (see Formula 4). The result is then used as the new soft walltime. The fourth technique—instead of using the average—keeps track of five most recent completed jobs. For each such job it computes the $walltime_{usage}$ and then chooses the maximum and multiplies the job's walltime estimate by this maximum (see Formula 5). It represents a conservative strategy, where the new soft walltime is calculated using the known relative accuracy of user's recent estimates. By choosing the maximum $walltime_{usage}$ (i.e., choosing a job where the difference between actual and estimated runtime was minimal), this technique aims to minimize the number of cases where the new soft walltime will be underestimated. At the same time, by ignoring older jobs it reflects aging and orients itself more on the recent user's workload characteristics—which is not the case when the average-based method is used instead.

$$walltime_{usage}(job_i) = \frac{runtime(job_i)}{walltime(job_i)} \tag{3}$$

$$soft\_walltime(job_i) = walltime(job_i) \cdot \frac{1}{i-1} \sum_{k=1}^{i-1} walltime_{usage}(job_k) \tag{4}$$

$$soft\_walltime(job_i) = walltime(job_i) \cdot \max_{i-5 \le k \le i-1} walltime_{usage}(job_k) \tag{5}$$

During our initial experiments, we have soon realized that out of these four techniques, the worst results are typically obtained by the average-based techniques (second and third technique). Therefore, in the remaining part of this paper we only use the first (runtime of last completed job) and the fourth prediction technique, depicting them as *last runtime* and *min. diff.*, respectively.

## 4   Experimental Evaluation

This section describes the results of our evaluation, where we use aforementioned prediction techniques to generate soft walltime limits. Before we proceed to the results of our simulations, we describe the workload traces used in our experiments and the simulation methodology.

---

[2] The system is configured to kill a job if it exceeds user's walltime estimate.

## 4.1  Workload Log Characteristics

In this work, we use eight different workloads coming from different systems with different parameters. Four workloads come from the Czech National distributed computing infrastructure. This infrastructure is managed by two major resource providers—CERIT-SC and MetaCentrum—each having its own job scheduler. We use three workload traces from CERIT-SC [3] system and one trace from MetaCentrum [17]. MetaCentrum_2013 trace includes 150 K jobs, while CERIT-SC_2013, CERIT-SC_2015 and CERIT-SC_2017 contain 257 K, 102 K and 252 K jobs, respectively. Remaining four workloads come from the Parallel Workloads Archive (PWA) [8]. We have used HPC2N, KTH SP2, CTC SP2 and SDSC SP2 traces that contain 202 K, 28 K, 77 K and 59 K jobs, respectively.

These workloads were selected because they represent very different systems. For example, both MetaCentrum and CERIT-SC are rather heterogeneous environments, providing access to several different clusters simultaneously. MetaCentrum_2013 workload trace comes from 14 clusters, CERIT-SC_2013 comes from 4 clusters while CERIT-SC_2015 and CERIT-SC_2017 come from 6 and 7 clusters, respectively. On the other hand, HPC2N, KTH SP2, CTC SP2 and SDSC SP2 traces each represent workloads coming from a single homogeneous cluster. Most importantly, these eight workloads exhibit very different *levels of accuracy* and different *variability* of users' runtime estimates. This is a very important factor which allows us to analyze how soft walltimes behave subject to either very imprecise or reasonably accurate estimates.

Figure 1 shows the cumulative distribution functions (CDF) of user estimates and actual runtimes for all eight data sets. Clearly, MetaCentrum_2013 and CERIT-SC_2013 traces have very poor estimates, where most users chose the default 24 h estimate. The situation is slightly better in CERIT-SC_2015 and CERIT-SC_2017 workloads because by that time the default 24 h estimate has been disabled by system administrators and users were forced to specify estimates upon job submissions. Still, the shape of the CDF resembles a staircase [29], which means that users preferred several common estimates, e.g., 2 h, 4 h, 24 h, 2 days or 1 week.

On the other hand, all workloads from PWA show better precision and variability of walltime estimates. It is also worth mentioning, that with the exception of HPC2N, these workloads do not contain jobs requesting walltime greater than 24 h, which is another major difference with respect to MetaCentrum and CERIT-SC traces.

## 4.2  Simulation Methodology

All experiments have been performed using Alea jobs scheduling simulator [13], with EASY backfilling as the scheduling algorithm [23]. The simulation code can be found at GitHub [1], while all traces can be obtained either from the Parallel Workloads Archive [8] or from the JSSPP's workloads archive [12].

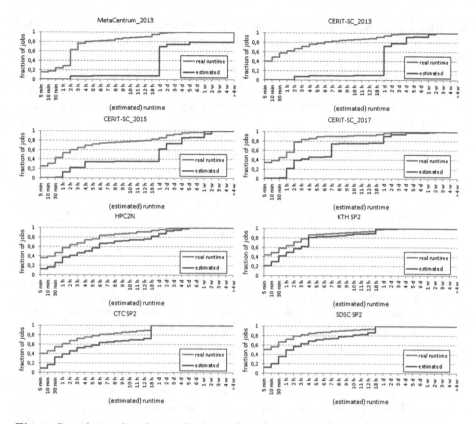

**Fig. 1.** Cumulative distribution functions (CDF) of actual and estimated job runtimes for all eight workloads.

**Perfect Estimates, User-Provided Estimates and Soft Walltimes.** The experiments have been conducted as follows. First, we have simulated workload execution using perfect estimates, i.e., actual job runtimes were used by EASY backfilling to determine job reservations and backfilling opportunities. This setup represented our *baseline ideal solution*, where EASY is performing "correct decisions" based on accurate information. In the second step, we have used the user-provided estimates (without using soft walltimes). This setup represented the *standard solution*, i.e., the common situation which is normal in systems where no additional walltime refinement is used. Finally, we have run the same experiment while using soft walltimes in the EASY backfilling. As discussed in Sect. 3, only the *last runtime* and the *min. diff.* soft walltime prediction techniques have been used because average-based prediction techniques did not work very well.

**Workload Replay and Dynamic Workload Adaptation.** It is a common practice to perform simulations by using job workloads in a static way. In such scenario, a given workload is "replayed" in the simulator using original job submission timestamps. Although such experiments allow for easy comparison of different simulation setups they are less likely to realistically "mimic" users interactions and behavior. As explained in [31], job submission times in a real system depend on how users react to the performance of previous jobs. Moreover, usually there are some logical structures of dependencies between jobs. It is therefore not very reasonable to use a workload "as is" with fixed (original) job submission timestamps, as the subsequent simulation may produce unrealistic scenarios with either too low or too high system loads, skewing the final results significantly.

Instead, dependency information and user behavior can be extracted from a workload trace, in terms of job batches, user sessions and think times between the completion of one batch and the submission of a subsequent batch. Then, each user's workload is divided into a sequence of dependent batches. During the simulation, these dependencies are preserved, and a new user's batch is submitted only when all its dependencies are satisfied (previous "parent" batches are completed). This creates the desired feedback effect, where job submission times are not dictated by the workload but are the result of the (simulated) scheduler-to-user interaction as users dynamically react to the actual performance of the system. At the same time, major characteristics of the workload including job properties or per-user job ordering are still preserved. More details can be found at [13,31].

In order to get reasonable results we use a compromise simulation scenario, combining both static and dynamic workloads. We use the dynamic approach of Zakay and Feitelson [31] with our two most recent workloads (CERIT-SC_2017 and CERIT-SC_2015). These workloads are "fresh", representing realistically the system that we are trying to optimize in practice. For the six remaining workloads we use the standard simulation practice, i.e., we use them statically.

**Result Analysis.** In case of both static and dynamic workloads we analyze the performance using two different approaches. First, we measure the overall impact of inaccurate walltimes and soft walltimes using the common average wait time [7] and the average slowdown [9] criteria. These results are discussed in Sect. 4.3. Next, we use detailed heatmaps [14] to better understand the impact of estimates and soft walltimes on jobs with respect to their CPU and runtime requirements. In a heatmap, a given metric is computed separately for each square of that heatmap. A square (or a bucket) on a heatmap is defined by its $x$ and $y$ coordinates and represents all jobs that fall into this category based on their CPU ($y$-axis) and runtime requirements ($x$-axis). Heatmaps are very useful visual aids allowing for quick and rather detailed result comparisons. These detailed results based on heatmaps are presented in Sect. 4.4. Furthermore, when the dynamic workload adaptation is used (CERIT-SC_2015/2017 workloads), we provide an additional analysis that measures the impact that soft walltimes have on individual jobs and users[3]. These additional results are also presented in Sect. 4.4. Finally, we conclude our experiments with the discussion in Sect. 4.5.

## 4.3   Overall Results

We start our evaluation by focusing on the overall impact that inaccurate estimates and soft walltimes have on the average wait time and slowdown. As the *baseline experiment* we always use the results obtained when simulating EASY backfilling using perfect estimates (i.e., estimate = runtime). Next we measure the improvement or deterioration of average wait time and slowdown. The improvement or deterioration is expressed as *percentage* and is computed using Formula 6, where $metric_{baseline}$ denotes the avg. wait time/slowdown of the baseline solution (perfect estimates) and $metric_x$ is the value of avg. wait time/slowdown of the solution where perfect estimates were replaced either with the user-provided estimates (*estimated*) or soft walltimes (either *last runtime* or *min. diff.*).

$$percentage = \frac{metric_{baseline} - metric_x}{metric_{baseline}/100} \qquad (6)$$

If a given metric is improved (i.e., avg. wait time/slowdown is decreased) then the resulting percentage is positive while a deterioration of a metric results in a negative percentage. It is worth noticing that positive percentage cannot exceed 100%, while negative percentage is not upper bounded[4]. The results of this experiment are shown in Fig. 2 (avg. wait time) and Fig. 3 (avg. slowdown), respectively. As discussed, for each workload trace we show the improvement/deterioration obtained with respect to the baseline solution[5].

Let us start with the average wait time. With the exception of HPC2N workload, the average wait times deteriorated when original user-provided estimates (*estimated*) were used compared to a solution computed using perfect estimates. Similarly, also the average slowdown of *estimated* deteriorated in all case, compared to the baseline scenario. As discussed, e.g., in Tsafrir's papers [29, 30], this is not surprising since less accurate and less variable estimates may worsen the performance.

---

[3] Unlike in the static scenario, user-oriented analysis makes a great sense when the workload is dynamically adapted.

[4] For example, if the result is 25% it means that, e.g., the original wait time was decreased by 25%. On the other hand, if the result is −300%, it means that the original wait time was increased by 300%, i.e., four times.

[5] The actual average wait times of the baseline solution were as follows: CERIT-SC_2015 (6.5 h), CERIT-SC_2017 (4.1 h), MetaCentrum_2013 (3.0 h), CERIT-SC_2013 (6.0 h), HPC2N (4.2 h), KTH SP2 (1.8 h), CTC SP2 (3.8 h) and SDSC SP2 (4.9 h). The average slowdowns of the baseline solution were following: CERIT-SC_2015 (249.9), CERIT-SC_2017 (127.9), MetaCentrum_2013 (115.5), CERIT-SC_2013 (620.7), HPC2N (143.2), KTH SP2 (105.8), CTC SP2 (49.9) and SDSC SP2 (72.8).

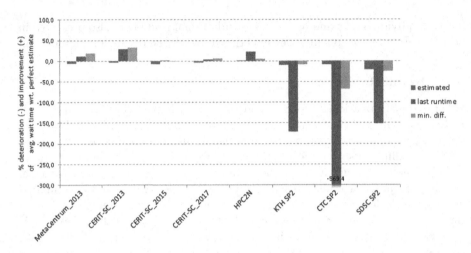

**Fig. 2.** Avg. wait time improvement (+) and deterioration (−) for all eight workloads.

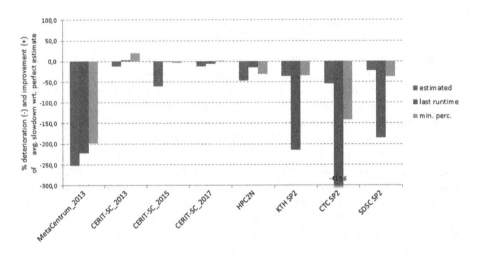

**Fig. 3.** Avg. slowdown improvement (+) and deterioration (−) for all eight workloads.

More interesting results are achieved by those two soft walltime-based prediction techniques (*last runtime* or *min. diff.*). In this case we are not only interested whether or not they improve/deteriorate the performance with respect to the baseline solution but more importantly we focus how good or bad are they with respect to (A) *estimated* solution and (B) each other. When the soft walltimes are constructed using *last runtime*, the results are better with respect to *estimated* in five workloads. In the remaining three workloads, using *last runtime* as the soft walltime prediction technique actually deteriorates the performance, both from the point of view of the avg. wait time and slowdown. The *min. diff.*

technique works better. It outperforms the *estimated* scenario in six workloads (both wait time and slowdown). Also, it outperforms the results of *last runtime* technique in six of eight workloads (both wait time and slowdown). Therefore, from now on we will only consider the *min. diff.* soft walltime prediction technique in the following experiments.

What these results show is that it certainly makes sense to consider soft walltimes in some cases. As can be seen, soft walltimes work best in the first five or six workloads (six, if only *min. diff.* is considered). We now try to answer the question why is it so. The main difference between the first five workloads and the remaining three (KTH SP2, CTC SP2 and SDSC SP2) is that all of them contain very long jobs that run/require more than 24 h. Also, all CERIT-SC/MetaCentrum-based workloads have very poor user-provided runtime estimates, compared to the remaining four traces. Clearly, the combination of long jobs and poor original estimates increases the chance that even trivial prediction technique such as *min. diff.* will produce a reasonable "mixture" of varying estimates that are very useful when "filling the holes" in the schedule[6].

Although our initial experiments shed some light on the problem, we now proceed to a more detailed analysis. So far, we have only used the average wait time/slowdown criteria which can be easily skewed by the long-tail effects of the underlying job wait time and slowdown distributions. Therefore, in the following section we use performance heatmaps [14] to better demonstrate the improving effect of soft walltimes.

## 4.4  Detailed Performance Analysis Using Heatmaps

This analysis uses two different types of heatmaps. The first type is used to show the distribution of jobs with respect to their actual runtime and CPU requirements, i.e., it shows which job classes (sizes) are the most common ones and which on the other hand are quite rare. The color scale of such heatmap represents the number of jobs belonging to a given "bucket".

The second type of heatmap is used to show the difference among average wait times of two different simulation setups. We compare the average wait time on a per "job bucket" basis. The color scale of such heatmap then shows the differences between the avg. wait times of the *baseline* solution and either *estimated* or *min. diff.* scenario. The result is either positive, negative or zero. A positive value (shades of red) represents an improvement with respect to the baseline solution (wait time of the baseline solution was higher), while a negative value represents a deterioration with respect to the baseline solution (shades of blue). A zero value represents no difference of average wait times (white color).

---

[6] With only few estimates used throughout the whole workload, backfilling has significantly decreased opportunity to fill these holes, because "most jobs look the same" and thus do not fit within available holes.

**Dynamic Workloads.** We start the discussion with our two dynamic workloads—CERIT-SC_2015/2017. The heatmaps for these workloads are presented in Figs. 4 and 5. Each such figure shows the job distribution heatmap (top), avg. job wait time difference heatmaps for *baseline* vs. *estimated* setup (middle) and *baseline* vs. *min. diff.*-based soft walltimes (bottom).

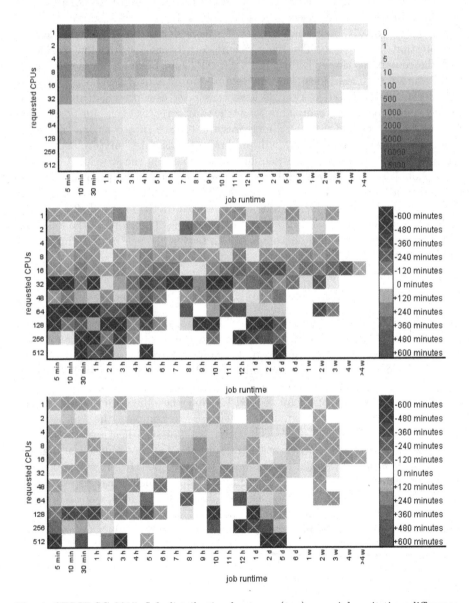

**Fig. 4.** CERIT-SC_2015. Job distribution heatmap (top), avg. job wait time difference heatmaps for *baseline* vs. *estimated* (middle) and *baseline* vs. *min. diff.* (bottom). (Color figure online)

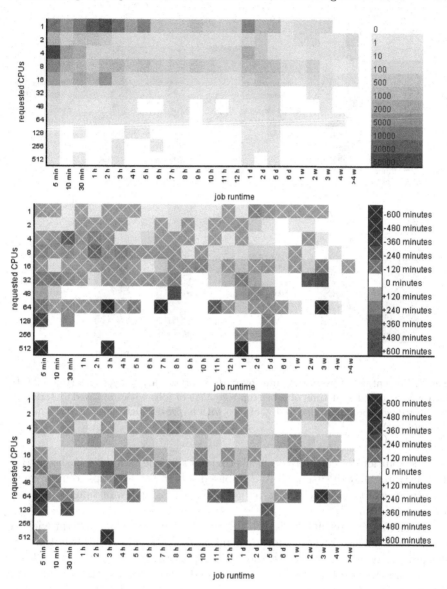

**Fig. 5.** CERIT-SC_2017. Job distribution heatmap (top), avg. job wait time difference heatmaps for *baseline* vs. *estimated* (middle) and *baseline* vs. *min. diff.* (bottom). (Color figure online)

As we can observe, the promising results related to soft walltimes that were observed in Sect. 4.3 are confirmed by the (bottom) heatmaps in Figs. 4 and 5. Here, the bottom heatmaps—showing the avg. wait time difference between baseline and soft walltime-based solution—are always "more red and less blue" than middle heatmaps, in which the difference between the baseline solution

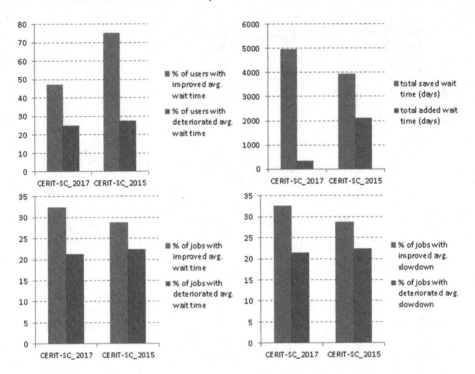

**Fig. 6.** Percentage of users with improved/deteriorated avg. wait times (top left), the total saved/added wait time of jobs (top right), % of jobs with improved/deteriorated avg. slowdown (bottom right) and % of jobs with improved/deteriorated avg. wait time (bottom left).

and the solution based solely on user-provided runtime estimates is shown. This demonstrates that the use of *min. diff.*-based soft walltimes helps to improve the performance of EASY backfilling, reducing the average job wait time significantly for most job "sizes".

Accompanying results related to the two dynamic workloads are provided in Fig. 6. Here we use several additional measurements (based on wait time and slowdown) to further illustrate the overall positive effect that soft walltimes create compared to the original user-provided estimates. Starting in the upper left corner and moving clockwise, the figure shows the percentage of users with improved/deteriorated average wait times, the total saved/added wait time of jobs in the system, the percentage of jobs with improved/deteriorated average slowdowns and finally the percentage of jobs with improved/deteriorated average wait times.

These results confirm, that soft walltimes improve the overall performance of the system. As the metrics indicate, many users now wait shorter and many jobs now have better wait times and slowdowns. As a result, the system minimizes overall waiting, as shown by the "total saved/added wait time" chart. Sure, every improvement comes with a price and we can see some performance deterioration for a fraction of jobs or users. However, the overall balance is always positive.

**Static Workloads.** Heatmap-based results for the remaining six static workloads are shown in Figs. 7, 8, 9, 10, 11 and 12. Again, the promising results of soft
walltimes that were observed for MetaCentrum_2013 and CERIT-SC_2013 workloads in Sect. 4.3 are confirmed by the heatmaps in Figs. 7 and 8. The improvement obtained by soft walltimes (bottom heatmaps) is significant compared to

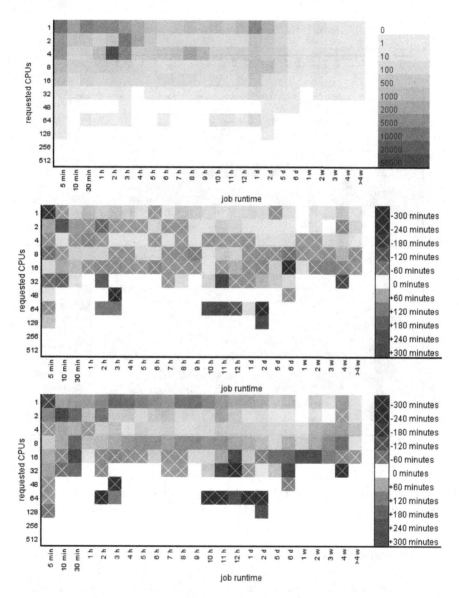

**Fig. 7.** MetaCentrum_2013. Job distribution heatmap (top), avg. job wait time difference heatmaps for *baseline* vs. *estimated* (middle) and *baseline* vs. *min. diff.* (bottom).

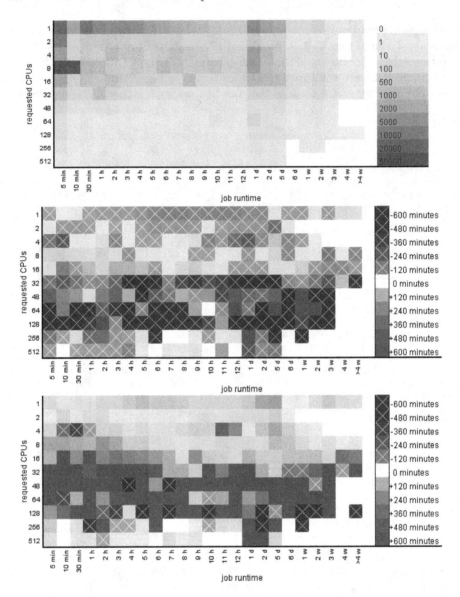

**Fig. 8.** CERIT-SC_2013. Job distribution heatmap (top), avg. job wait time difference heatmaps for *baseline* vs. *estimated* (middle) and *baseline* vs. *min. diff.* (bottom).

the middle heatmaps which show the difference between baseline (perfect) solution and solution based on the inaccurate user-provided runtime estimates.

A different situation is visible in case of HPC2N (Fig. 9) and KTH SP2 (Fig. 10) workloads. Here we see that soft walltime-based solutions (bottom heatmap) slightly improve average wait times for jobs requiring small amounts

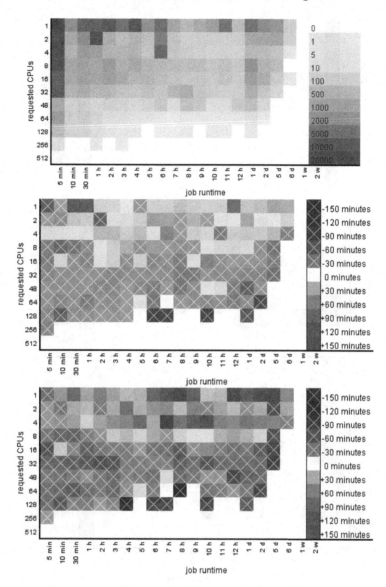

**Fig. 9.** HPC2N. Job distribution heatmap (top), avg. job wait time difference heatmaps for *baseline* vs. *estimated* (middle) and *baseline* vs. *min. diff.* (bottom).

of CPUs. The effect is more visible for HPC2N. On the other hand, wait times of longer and more CPU demanding jobs are slightly increased (compared to the middle heatmap). As the top heatmaps reveal, both HPC2N and KTH SP2 have large job concentrations in the upper half of the heatmap, meaning that many jobs in the workload require only up to 32 CPUs. These are the same parts where the improvement can be observed. Together, it help us to understand the

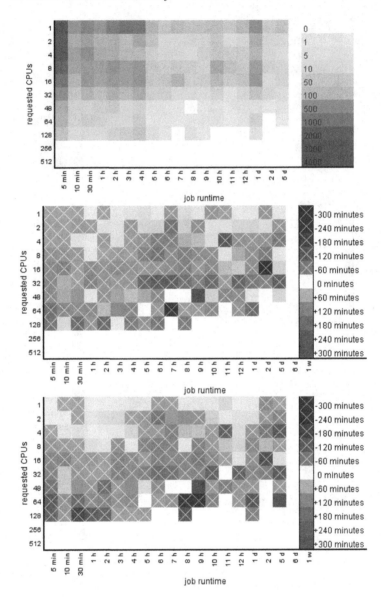

**Fig. 10.** KTH SP2. Job distribution heatmap (top), avg. job wait time difference heatmaps for *baseline* vs. *estimated* (middle) and *baseline* vs. *min. diff.* (bottom).

average wait time results seen in the Fig. 2, where the setup involving soft wall-times (*min. diff.*) slightly outperformed the setup using user-provided estimates.

Finally, Figs. 11 and 12 (SDSC SP2 and CTC SP2 workloads) show the two situations in which soft walltimes based on *min. diff.* predictions do not work at all. In case of SDSC SP2, setup involving soft walltimes behaves similarly to the

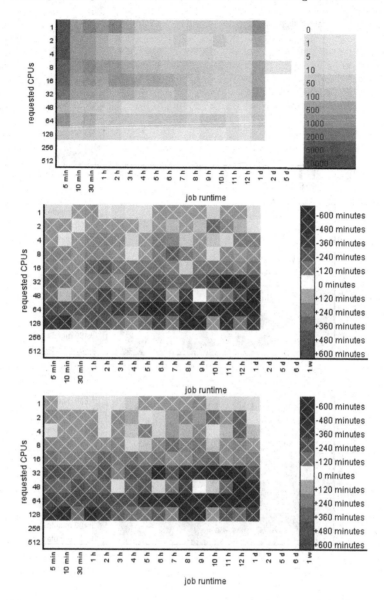

**Fig. 11.** SDSC SP2. Job distribution heatmap (top), avg. job wait time difference heatmaps for *baseline* vs. *estimated* (middle) and *baseline* vs. *min. diff.* (bottom).

one relying on user-provided estimates, which corresponds to the observations in Fig. 2. In case of CTC SP2, the use of soft walltimes deteriorates the performance for nearly all job sizes, as demonstrates the bottom heatmap in Fig. 12. Again, this heatmap corresponds to the bad average wait time result observed in Fig. 2.

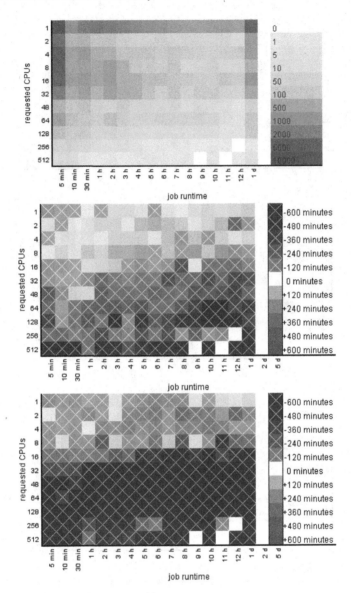

**Fig. 12.** CTC SP2. Job distribution heatmap (top), avg. job wait time difference heatmaps for *baseline* vs. *estimated* (middle) and *baseline* vs. *min. diff.* (bottom).

## 4.5   Discussion

The experiments presented in Sects. 4.3 and 4.4 clearly demonstrated that for some workloads (and actual systems) even trivially constructed soft walltimes may represent an interesting option compared to the imprecise, coarse-grained user-provided estimates. On the other hand, it seem very likely that systems that (A) have reasonably variable user runtime estimates, and (B) do not contain long jobs, will not gain much improvement from presented techniques. This is not surprising, because such workloads already offer a lot of backfilling opportunities. Perhaps, it will be worth trying soft walltimes in such systems if some more accurate prediction method is available.

One of the interesting features of soft walltimes is that they do not directly rely on a user's (un)willingness to provide reasonable guesses. In a saturated system, where users compete for resources it would be very probable that some users would try to *cheat the scheduler*, by providing long walltime limits and (very) short soft walltimes. Without further "anti-cheating" mechanisms these users would be favored by the backfilling and would degrade both the accuracy and fairness of the system. Therefore, the use of soft walltimes provided by some "black box solution" will be more safe and fair than if users are allowed to directly specify both walltimes and soft walltimes. Sure, since prediction techniques usually use historic information concerning job runtimes, users can still "game" the prediction system in an indirect fashion, e.g., by submitting large numbers of very short jobs before submitting a very long computation. It is then up to the system administrator to develop some form of an anti-cheating policy.

## 5    Conclusion and Future Work

In this paper, we have analyzed the suitability and impact of using soft walltimes in parallel job scheduling. Soft walltimes clearly represent an interesting solution for systems where users are either unable or unwilling to provide reasonably heterogeneous and/or accurate estimates. In such systems even very simple runtime prediction techniques (like those used in this paper) can significantly improve the performance of the scheduler through increasing the portfolio of jobs suitable for backfilling.

On the other hand, our simulation results suggest that soft walltimes do not improve the performance in systems where the user-provided runtime estimates are already reasonably accurate or at least exhibit great variability. In such cases our simple prediction techniques fail to deliver better solutions.

In the future, it would be very interesting to analyze whether more advanced prediction techniques can deliver better performance. Here, it is important to define what "better perfomance" means. Using our own experience as well as the observations of other researchers it is highly likely that "better estimates" will not always produce, e.g., better average wait time or slowdown. This is obvious from the fact, that there are several examples (workloads) where the use of perfect estimates (estimate = runtime) leads to worse average wait time and/or slowdown, compared to the setup where the user-provided inaccurate estimates are used instead. However, there are other important metrics that can benefit from improved estimates. For example, the reliability of predicted start times of jobs in a queue will improve if more accurate estimates are used. For some use cases this improved predictability may represent more important role than, e.g., the wait time.

Last but not least, we see another promising direction of using soft walltimes in systems with heterogeneous resources that have (significantly) different speeds of CPUs, GPUs and I/O devices. MetaCentrum and CERIT-SC represent such heterogeneous systems where different clusters are of different age and use different CPU/GPU architectures with big differences in processing and I/O speeds (local SSD scratch disks vs. local HDD vs. shared file system). In such systems, it would be interesting to adapt user-provided estimates and/or soft walltimes with respect to the actual machine being used. Our observations suggest that the runtime of CPU/GPU intensive applications significantly decreases on modern CPUs/GPUs while I/O intensive applications benefit from using fast local SSD scratch disks. It seems promising to use a prediction technique to adapt soft walltimes dynamically according to the performance characteristics of available resources and expected application's CPU/GPU and I/O demands.

**Acknowledgments.** We kindly acknowledge the support and computational resources provided by the MetaCentrum under the program LM2015042 and the CERIT Scientific Cloud under the program LM2015085, provided under the programme "Projects of Large Infrastructure for Research, Development, and Innovations" and the project Reg. No. CZ.02.1.01/0.0/0.0/16_013/0001797 co-funded by the Ministry of Education, Youth and Sports of the Czech Republic. We also highly appreciate the access to the workload traces provided by the Parallel Workloads Archive, MetaCentrum and CERIT-SC.

# References

1. Alea 4: Job scheduling simulator, February 2018. https://github.com/aleasimulator
2. Balasundaram, V., Fox, G., Kennedy, K., Kremer, U.: A static performance estimator to guide data partitioning decisions. ACM SIGPLAN Not. **26**(7), 213–223 (1991)
3. CERIT Scientific Cloud, February 2018. http://www.cerit-sc.cz
4. Chiang, S.-H., Arpaci-Dusseau, A., Vernon, M.K.: The impact of more accurate requested runtimes on production job scheduling performance. In: Feitelson, D.G., Rudolph, L., Schwiegelshohn, U. (eds.) JSSPP 2002. LNCS, vol. 2537, pp. 103–127. Springer, Heidelberg (2002). https://doi.org/10.1007/3-540-36180-4_7
5. Devarakonda, M.V., Iyer, R.K.: Predictability of process resource usage: a measurement based study on UNIX. IEEE Trans. Softw. Eng. **15**(12), 1579–1586 (1989)
6. Downey, A.B.: Predicting queue times on space-sharing parallel computers. In: 11th International Parallel Processing Symposium, pp. 209–218 (1997)
7. Ernemann, C., Hamscher, V., Yahyapour, R.: Benefits of global Grid computing for job scheduling. In: GRID '04: Proceedings of the 5th IEEE/ACM International Workshop on Grid Computing, pp. 374–379. IEEE (2004)
8. Feitelson, D.G.: Parallel workloads archive, February 2018. http://www.cs.huji.ac.il/labs/parallel/workload/
9. Feitelson, D.G., Rudolph, L., Schwiegelshohn, U., Sevcik, K.C., Wong, P.: Theory and practice in parallel job scheduling. In: Feitelson, D.G., Rudolph, L. (eds.) JSSPP 1997. LNCS, vol. 1291, pp. 1–34. Springer, Heidelberg (1997). https://doi.org/10.1007/3-540-63574-2_14

10. Feitelson, D.G., Weil, A.M.: Utilization and predictability in scheduling the IBM SP2 with backfilling. In: 12th International Parallel Processing Symposium, pp. 542–546. IEEE (1998)
11. Guim, F., Corbalan, J., Labarta, J.: Prediction f based models for evaluating backfilling scheduling policies. In: Eighth International Conference on Parallel and Distributed Computing, Applications and Technologies (PDCAT 2007), pp. 9–17. IEEE (2007)
12. Klusáček, D.: Workload traces from metacentrum and CERIT Scientific Cloud, February 2018. http://jsspp.org/workload/
13. Klusáček, D., Tóth, Š., Podolníková, G.: Complex job scheduling simulations with Alea 4. In: Ninth EAI International Conference on Simulation Tools and Techniques (SimuTools 2016), pp. 124–129. ACM (2016)
14. Krakov, D., Feitelson, D.G.: Comparing performance heatmaps. In: Desai, N., Cirne, W. (eds.) JSSPP 2013. LNCS, vol. 8429, pp. 42–61. Springer, Heidelberg (2014). https://doi.org/10.1007/978-3-662-43779-7_3
15. Kumar, R., Vadhiyar, S.: Prediction of queue waiting times for metascheduling on parallel batch systems. In: Cirne, W., Desai, N. (eds.) Job Scheduling Strategies for Parallel Processing. LNCS, vol. 8828, pp. 108–128. Springer (2014)
16. Bailey Lee, C., Schwartzman, Y., Hardy, J., Snavely, A.: Are user runtime estimates inherently inaccurate? In: Feitelson, D.G., Rudolph, L., Schwiegelshohn, U. (eds.) JSSPP 2004. LNCS, vol. 3277, pp. 253–263. Springer, Heidelberg (2005). https://doi.org/10.1007/11407522_14
17. MetaCentrum, February 2018. http://www.metacentrum.cz/
18. Mu'alem, A.W., Feitelson, D.G.: Utilization, predictability, workloads, and user runtime estimates in scheduling the IBM SP2 with backfilling. IEEE Trans. Parallel Distrib. Syst. **12**(6), 529–543 (2001)
19. Nurmi, D., Brevik, J., Wolski, R.: QBETS: queue bounds estimation from time series. In: Frachtenberg, E., Schwiegelshohn, U. (eds.) JSSPP 2007. LNCS, vol. 4942, pp. 76–101. Springer, Heidelberg (2008). https://doi.org/10.1007/978-3-540-78699-3_5
20. PBS Works. PBS Professional 14.2, Administrator's Guide, February 2018. http://www.pbsworks.com
21. Sarkar, V.: Determining average program execution times and their variance. In: ACM SIGPLAN Conference on Programming Language Design and Implementation, pp. 298–312 (1989)
22. Seneviratne, S., Witharana, S.: A survey on methodologies for runtime prediction on grid environments. In: 7th International Conference on Information and Automation for Sustainability, pp. 1–6. IEEE (2014)
23. Skovira, J., Chan, W., Zhou, H., Lifka, D.: The EASY — LoadLeveler API project. In: Feitelson, D.G., Rudolph, L. (eds.) JSSPP 1996. LNCS, vol. 1162, pp. 41–47. Springer, Heidelberg (1996). https://doi.org/10.1007/BFb0022286
24. Smith, W., Foster, I., Taylor, V.: Predicting application run times using historical information. In: Feitelson, D.G., Rudolph, L. (eds.) Job Scheduling Strategies for Parallel Processing. LNCS, vol. 1459, pp. 122–142. Springer, Heidelberg (1998)

25. Smith, W., Taylor, V., Foster, I.: Using run-time predictions to estimate queue wait times and improve scheduler performance. In: Feitelson, D.G., Rudolph, L. (eds.) JSSPP 1999. LNCS, vol. 1659, pp. 202–219. Springer, Heidelberg (1999). https://doi.org/10.1007/3-540-47954-6_11
26. Soft walltime documentation, February 2018. https://pbspro.atlassian.net/wiki/spaces/PD/pages/42532871/PP-482+Soft+Walltime
27. Talby, D., Feitelson, D.G.: Supporting priorities and improving utilization of the IBM SP scheduler using slack-based backfilling. In: IPPS 1999/SPDP 1999: Proceedings of the 13th International Symposium on Parallel Processing and the 10th Symposium on Parallel and Distributed Processing, pp. 513–517. IEEE Computer Society (1999)
28. Tang, W., Desai, N., Buettner, D., Lan, Z.: Analyzing and adjusting user runtime estimates to improve job scheduling on the Blue Gene/P. In: IEEE International Symposium on Parallel and Distributed Processing (IPDPS), pp. 1–11. IEEE (2010)
29. Tsafrir, D.: Using inaccurate estimates accurately. In: Frachtenberg, E., Schwiegelshohn, U. (eds.) JSSPP 2010. LNCS, vol. 6253, pp. 208–221. Springer, Heidelberg (2010). https://doi.org/10.1007/978-3-642-16505-4_12
30. Tsafrir, D., Etsion, Y., Feitelson, D.G.: Modeling user runtime estimates. In: Feitelson, D., Frachtenberg, E., Rudolph, L., Schwiegelshohn, U. (eds.) JSSPP 2005. LNCS, vol. 3834, pp. 1–35. Springer, Heidelberg (2005). https://doi.org/10.1007/11605300_1
31. Zakay, N., Feitelson, D.G.: Preserving user behavior characteristics in trace-based simulation of parallel job scheduling. In: 22nd Modeling, Analysis and Simulation of Computer and Telecommunications Systems (MASCOTS), pp. 51–60 (2014)

# Reducing the Human-in-the-Loop Component of the Scheduling of Large HTC Workloads

Frédéric Azevedo, Luc Gombert, and Frédéric Suter[(✉)]

IN2P3 Computing Center, CNRS, Lyon-Villeurbanne, France
{frederic.azevedo,luc.gombert,frederic.suter}@cc.in2p3.fr

**Abstract.** A common characteristic to major physics experiments is an ever increasing need of computing resources to process experimental data and generate simulated data. The IN2P3 Computing Center provides its 2,500 users with about 35,000 cores and processes millions of jobs every month. This workload is composed of a vast majority of sequential jobs that corresponds to Monte-Carlo simulations and related analysis made on data produced on the Large Hadron Collider at CERN.

To schedule such a workload under specific constraints, the CC-IN2P3 relied for 20 years on an in-house job and resource management system complemented by an operation team who can directly act on the decisions made by the job scheduler and modify them. This system has been replaced in 2011 but legacy rules of thumb remained. Combined to other rules motivated by production constraints, they may act against the job scheduler optimizations and force the operators to apply more corrective actions than they should.

In this experience report from a production system, we describe the decisions made since the end of 2016 to either transfer some of the actions done by operators to the job scheduler or make these actions become unnecessary. The physical partitioning of resources in distinct pools has been replaced by a logical partitioning that leverages scheduling queues. Then some historical constraints, such as quotas, have been relaxed. For instance, the number of concurrent jobs from a given user group allowed to access a specific resource, e.g., a storage subsystem, has been progressively increased. Finally, the computation of the fair-share by the job scheduler has been modified to be less detrimental to small groups whose jobs have a low priority. The preliminary but promising results coming from these modifications constitute the beginning of a long-term activity to change the operation procedures applied to the computing infrastructure of the IN2P3 Computing Center.

## 1 Introduction

In the field of high-energy and astroparticle physics, detectors, satellites, telescopes, and numerical simulations of physical processes produce massive amounts of data. The comparison of these experimental and simulated data allows physicists to validate or disprove theories and led to major scientific discoveries over

© Springer Nature Switzerland AG 2019
D. Klusáček et al. (Eds.): JSSPP 2018, LNCS 11332, pp. 39–60, 2019.
https://doi.org/10.1007/978-3-030-10632-4_3

the last decade. For instance, in 2012, the ATLAS [10] and CMS [11] experiments running on the Large Hadron Collider (LHC) at CERN, both observed a new particle which is consistent with the Higgs boson predicted by the Standard Model. These observations confirmed a theory of the origin of mass of subatomic particles which was awarded the Nobel Prize in physics in 2013. In 2016, the LIGO and VIRGO scientific collaborations announced the first observation of gravitational waves [13] which confirmed the last remaining unproven prediction of general relativity.

The next decade will see the beginning of major projects that will allow astroparticle physicists to address the most pressing questions about the structure and evolution of the universe and the objects in it. From 2022, the Large Synoptic Survey Telescope (LSST) will conduct a 10-year survey of the sky to produce the largest catalog of celestial objects ever built while the Euclid spatial telescope aims at drawing a 3D map of hundreds of millions galaxies from 2020.

A common characteristic to all these physics experiments is an ever increasing need of computing and storage resources to process and store experimental data and generate simulated data. Moreover, the sheer amount of data produced by physics experiments enforces the distribution of data and computations across a worldwide federation of computing centers.

The Computing Center of the National Institute of Nuclear Physics and Particle Physics (CC-IN2P3) [12] is one of the largest academic computing centers in France. It provides its more than 2,500 users from 80 scientific collaborations with about 35,000 cores and 340PB of storage. The reliability and high availability of the CC-IN2P3 allows it to achieve an utilization of these resources above 90%. In particular, the CC-IN2P3 is one of the twelve Tier-1 centers in the Worldwide LHC Computing Grid (WLCG) engaged in the primary processing of the data produced by the LHC and one of the only four centers that provide storage and processing resources for all four experiments installed on the accelerator.

This participation in the WLCG strongly influences the organization and the operation of the computing at the CC-IN2P3. It also defines and shapes the workload that is executed. Indeed, the four LHC experiments alone have used up to 75% of the allocated resources. In 2018, they represented 58% of the allocations, as the needs expressed by other experiments have been increasing.

The main characteristic of the CC-IN2P3's workload is that it is a High Throughput Computing (HTC) workload composed of a vast majority of sequential jobs. It mainly corresponds to Monte-Carlo simulation jobs and related data analysis made on the data produced at the LHC. We observed an increasing share of multi-core jobs (i.e., using several cores within the limits of a single node) in the workload over the last three years. Most of these multi-core jobs also run Monte-Carlo simulations but allow physicists to share some libraries and data structure and thus reduce the memory footprint. Finally, HPC jobs (e.g., using MPI or GPUs) are executed on a distinct set of nodes, which only represents a small fraction of the overall computing capacity of the CC-IN2P3.

The requirements of the main experiments running at the CC-IN2P3 influence the performance metrics the job scheduling system has to optimize. Indeed, the resource allocation procedure differs from that of traditional HPC centers where scientific collaborations usually submit a research proposal which includes a request for an *envelope of cores.hours* to use during a limited time period. For a Tier-1 center of the WLCG such as the CC-IN2P3, resource requests are expressed as pledges for a given *computing power* expressed in HS06 [9]. The computing center is then committed to provide enough resources to answer to those pledges. Moreover, the accounting is made with regard to the actual CPU usage of a job rather than on its duration. This specific allocation procedure has been extended beyond the four LHC experiments to all the groups computing at the CC-IN2P3. The main objectives for the batch scheduling system are thus to ensure a fair sharing [4] of the resources according to the different pledges and to guarantee that all the pledges are respected. These objectives are translated into priorities and quotas assigned to jobs and user groups.

Scheduling also has to take into account the data-driven nature of the executed jobs. Several experiments running at CC-IN2P3 make a heavy use of the different storage subsystems the center provides (e.g., GPFS, HPSS, iRODS). To prevent the saturation of a storage subsystem and a failure which could have a cascading impact on the execution of the workload, additional conservative quotas are assigned to groups to limit the number of concurrent running jobs.

To schedule such a peculiar workload with regard to the aforementioned constraints and objectives, the CC-IN2P3 developed and maintained its own in-house job and resource management system for nearly 20 years. The development of the *Batch Queuing System* (BQS) started in 1992 and was initially based on NASA's *Network Queuing System* (NQS). This system has been tailored to suit the specific needs of the computing center and its major users. For instance, it was possible to "program" the scheduler to meet the production objectives expressed by the different experiments. Moreover, the respect of a fair sharing of the resources among the scientific groups and accounting mechanisms to ensure the respect of the pledges were part of the initial design.

The job and resource management system is complemented by a team dedicated to the operation of the computing infrastructure that adds an important "human-in-the-loop" component to the scheduling of the workload. Indeed, the role of the operators is not limited to reacting to incidents related to either resources or jobs. They can also directly act on the decisions made by the job scheduler and modify them. For instance, an operator can manually boost or lower the priority of a job/user/group or change the allocations of resources to a given queue in a proactive way.

The decision to stop the development of BQS was taken in 2011. It had become too costly in terms of human resources over the years. Since then, the job and resource management system of the CC-IN2P3 is Univa Grid Engine [14]. However, some legacy rules of thumb from the operation of BQS remained and add to the different rules motivated by the constraints on the hardware and software resources and the respect of pledges. This accumulation of rules sometimes acts against the job scheduler optimizations and forces the operators to apply more corrective actions than they should.

In this experience report from a production system, we describe the decisions made since the end of 2016 to transfer some the actions done by operators to the job scheduling system or simply make these actions become unnecessary. The objective is to improve the job scheduling decisions, especially for small user groups and optimize the resource utilization, while minimizing the "human-in-the-loop" component in such decisions Three complementary modifications have already been implemented which deal with: (i) the partitioning of resources; (ii) the quotas assigned to the different user groups; and (iii) the computation of the fair-share by the job scheduler.

The remaining of this paper is organized as follows. First, we describe how large HTC workloads are processed at the CC-IN2P3 in Sect. 2 by detailing its computing infrastructure and scheduling and resource allocation procedures and characterizing the executed workload. Then, in Sect. 3, we motivate, present, and illustrate the benefits, be they an optimization of the scheduling and/or a reduction of the operation costs, for each of the three proposed modifications. Section 4 concludes this experience report and details future work directions.

## 2 Scheduling Large HTC Workloads at CC-IN2P3

### 2.1 Organization and Management of the Computing Infrastructure

As mentioned in the introduction, the CC-IN2P3 provides its users with about 35,000 *virtual* cores (i.e., hyper-threading is activated on physical cores). More precisely, and at the time of writing of this article, this computing infrastructure is made of 816 nodes whose characteristics are given in Table 1.

**Table 1.** Characteristics of the nodes in the CC-IN2P3's computing farm.

| Model | #Nodes | #vCores/Node | #vCores |
|---|---|---|---|
| Intel Xeon E5-2650 v4@2.20 GHz | 232 | 48 | 11,136 |
| Intel Xeon Silver 4114@2.20 GHz | 240 | 40 | 9,600 |
| Intel Xeon E5-2680 v2@2.80 GHz | 149 | 40 | 5,960 |
| Intel Xeon E5-2680 v3@2.50 GHz | 123 | 48 | 5,904 |
| Intel Xeon E5-2670 0@2.60 GHz | 72 | 32 | 2,304 |
| **Total** | **816** | | **34,904** |

Due to the recent upgrade of the default Operating System from Scientific Linux 6 to CentOS 7, this set of nodes is currently split into two distinct partitions of respectively 768 and 48 nodes. This allows the user groups that chose to not migrate their codes to get access to some resources. Nodes were progressively moved from one partition to the other from June 2017 to June 2018 as shown by Fig. 1. This variation in the size of the partitions and the set of user groups allowed to access each partition had an impact on several aspects of the scheduling process. We will highlight some of the consequences of this migration in the characterization of the workload given in Sect. 2.3.

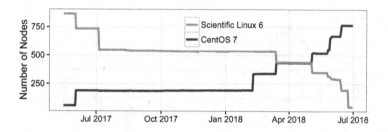

**Fig. 1.** Transition from the Scientific Linux 6 Operating System to CentOS 7.

In addition to these nodes that are dedicated to the execution of the HTC workload, the CC-IN2P3 also offers resources for parallel (512 cores without hyper-threading in 16 nodes), GPU-based (32 NVIDIA K80 GPUs and 128 cores in 8 nodes), and large memory (a node with 40 cores and 1.5 TB of memory) jobs, and five nodes dedicated to interactive jobs.

These computing resources are managed by Univa Grid Engine (UGE v8.4.4) whose scheduling algorithm is an implementation of the *Fair Share Scheduler* first described in [5]. Its principle is to assign priorities to all the unscheduled jobs to determine their order of execution. These priorities derive from three fundamental policies. The first policy is related to the *entitlement* of a job to access resources. It relies on the implementation of the *Share Tree* policy which defines this entitlement of a job according to the previous resource usage of a user/project/group. The administrators of the systems first define a total number of *tickets* which basically corresponds to a virtualized view of the complete set of resources managed by the system. This total number of tickets is then distributed among groups (and then among sub-projects, users, and eventually jobs). In the configuration used at CC-IN2P3, the different shares are proportional to the resource pledges expressed by the different user groups.

When a given group *A* does not use its allocated share, pending jobs of other groups are allowed to use the corresponding resources. The group with the least accumulated past usage has the highest priority in that case. However, when group *A* starts to submit jobs again, a compensation mechanism is triggered to allow this group to reach back its target share. Two parameters control the behavior of this policy, illustrated by Fig. 2. The *half-life* specifies how UGE forgets about the past usage of a given group. This parameter thus acts on the selection of groups allowed to benefit of the resources left unused by another group. The second parameter is the *compensation factor* that limits how fast a group will reach back its target share. The higher the value, the more reactive to variations in the workload the system will be. The current values used at CC-IN2P3 are 2,160 for the half-life and 2 for the compensation factor.

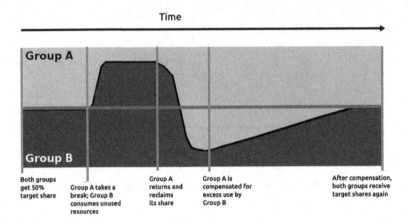

**Fig. 2.** Example of the Share-tree policy applied to two user groups allowed to use a half of the resources each.

The second policy implemented by UGE corresponds to the expression of the urgency of a job and defines some weights in the computation of the priority of the job. This urgency is decomposed in three components. First, the closer a job is to its deadline (if one has been specified at submission time, which is not the case at CC-IN2P3), the higher its priority will be. Second, the priority will also increase along with the waiting time of the job in the scheduling queue. Finally, a higher priority will be given to jobs that request expensive resources. For instance, at CC-IN2P3, resources are organized in queues whose characteristics are given in Table 2. These queues mainly differs by the maximum duration, both in terms of wallclock and CPU times, of the jobs, the available memory and scratch disk space, and the type of jobs, i.e., sequential or multi-core. In the current configuration, a greater weight is given to the multi-core queues, which are thus seen as more "expensive resources" than sequential queues.

**Table 2.** Upper bound on resources usage of the different batch scheduling queues.

| Queue | CPU time (in hours) | Walltime (in hours) | Memory (in GB) | Disk space (in GB) | #vCores |
|---|---|---|---|---|---|
| huge | 72 | 86 | 10 | 110 | 10,337 |
| long | 48 | 58 | 4 | 30 | 31,040 |
| longlasting | 168 | 192 | 4 | 30 | 3,996 |
| mc_huge | 72 | 86 | 8 | 30 | 9,336 |
| mc_long | 48 | 58 | 3.6 | 30 | 34,752 |
| mc_longlasting | 202 | 226 | 3 | 30 | 20,416 |

The sum of the maximum numbers of virtual cores that each queue can use is more than 2.86 times the actual number of available cores. This guarantees the highest possible utilization of the resources but also prevents the saturation of queues. Any type of job thus has a good chance to access resources, hence increasing the quality of service experienced by the users, who are not advised to specify a queue on submission. They are encouraged to express job requirements instead and let the scheduling system select the most appropriate queue.

The configuration of these queues also illustrates the operational priorities of the CC-IN2P3. We can see that the mc_* queues dedicated to multi-core jobs are allowed to access much more cores than the queues reserved to sequential jobs. This confirms the higher priority given to multi-core jobs which now represent a large fraction of the CPU consumption as the characterization of the workload given in Sect. 2.3 will show. We also note that jobs are not really distinguished by their execution time in this configuration. Indeed, the huge and mc_huge queues are primarily intended to jobs that need more memory or disk space. Moreover, the access to the longlasting queues is limited to certain user groups. Then, the bulk of the workload is directed to the long and mc_long queues. The rationale is to simplify the computation of the fair-share by the job scheduler whose respect is the main operational objective. However, this also calls for good estimations of job duration. Bad estimate can have two drawbacks. First, it may be harmful to the scheduler as it has to cope with important discrepancies between the "estimated" and actual duration of the jobs. Second, short jobs submitted by small groups whose priority is low with regard to the global fair-share policy may be severely delayed. Indeed, their short duration is not translated in an increase of their priority. As we will see in Sect. 2.3, estimations are not always provided or automatically defined and are usually far for being accurate.

The last component in the computation of job priorities by UGE is the capacity for users to manually specify a POSIX priority at submission which only acts as another weighting factor in the formula used to determine the overall scheduling priority of the job.

In addition to these policies implemented by the job and resource management system, a last configuration parameter has a strong influence on scheduling. This is the definition of limitations as *Resource Quota Sets* (RQS). These limitations are expressed as a maximal number of virtual cores (or slots in the UGE terminology) that can access a given hardware of software resource and thus be allowed to enter the system. They are applied at two levels. Global limitations are applied to all groups and jobs indifferently. Such limits are classically used to define resource pools (e.g., depending on the operating system running), prevent the saturation of a storage or database service, or are related to the number of available license tokens for commercial software.

In the specific configuration of the CC-IN2P3 system, extra RQS are applied to groups to either limit the number of concurrent jobs or the number of jobs accessing a given resource. The former is used as a way to enforce the respect of the resource pledges expressed by each group by averaging their estimated consumption over each quarter of the year. The latter corresponds to the implementation of a conservative approach to further prevent the saturation of sensitive storage subsystems such as a shared parallel file system.

## 2.2   Resource Allocation Procedure

Every year in September, the representative of each of the scientific collaborations using the CC-IN2P3 is asked to pledge resources for the next year. Each group provides an estimation of its needs in terms of computing and storage on each of the available subsystems. While the large collaborations such as those of the LHC experiments have a well defined and planned definition of their requirements at a worldwide scale, smaller groups usually define their needs from their consumption of the previous year with an empirically estimated delta.

The accuracy of these pledges is critical for two reasons. First, the sum of the expressed requirements, combined to the available budget, define, after an arbitration process, the purchase of new hardware to ensure that the CC-IN2P3 can fulfill its primary mission and serve all the experiments. This is another major difference with traditional HPC centers that buy and host the biggest affordable supercomputer and then arbitrate the demands with regard to the capacity of this machine. Second, the pledges define the Resource Quota Sets applied to each group and thus have a direct impact on job scheduling.

The allocation of computing resources works as follows. Each group expresses its pledge as an amount of work to be done during each quarter of the year. This amount is given in *Normalized HS06.hours*, a unit coming from the High Energy Physics community. It corresponds to the normalization of the results of the HS06 benchmark [9] on the different types of nodes in the computing infrastructure to take node heterogeneity into account multiplied by a number of hours.

The accumulation of all the required numbers of HS06.hours defines the computing power the CC-IN2P3 has to deliver. Once arbitration has been done, the respective share of this total number that has to be allocated to each group is computed. Then this share is converted into a number of virtual cores needed to process this amount of work in a year. Finally, this number of virtual cores defines a consumption objective used by the job scheduler to compute its fair-share.

## 2.3   Characterization of the Workload

We analyzed the workload processed at CC-IN2P3 over ten weeks from March 29, 2018 to June 12, 2018. This corresponds to the period between two scheduled maintenance shutdowns of the computing center. Job submissions are blocked a day before the maintenance in order to drain the scheduling queues while jobs are progressively allowed into the system after the maintenance to prevent stress on the storage subsystems.

We extracted and combined information on jobs from three tables of the Accounting and Reporting Console (ARCo) provided by Univa Grid Engine:

- The sge_job table contains basic information about jobs such as the job id, the user who submitted it and its group, or the submission date;

- The sge_job_usage table contains information about the resource usage made by a job, including its beginning and end date, the number of cores on which the job has been executed, its memory consumption, or its exit status;
- The sge_job_request table stores key-value pairs that correspond to the different resource requests made by jobs, such as the requested number of cores or memory, an estimation of the walltime, the specification of a given queue, or the need for a specific storage subsystem.

We performed a first processing of these database extracts to solve two major issues related to the way UGE stores information into ARCo. First, ARCo creates several entries for jobs whose execution spans over more than a day. For instance, for a job starting on April 25th at 5 PM and ending on April 26th at 11 AM, two entries will be created, one for April 25th from 5 PM to 12 AM and one for April 26th from 12 AM to 11 AM. Moreover, only the last entry will log the total runtime of the job, the other ones leaving that field to 0. We thus had to merge all the entries for such long jobs into a single one. Second, the CPU consumption is not stored in seconds but in *normalized HS06*, the unit used for resource pledges. A normalization factor is applied that depends on the node onto which the job has been executed to take into account the heterogeneity of the computing nodes. This factor ranges from 9.7 to 11.3. For each job in the workload, we found out the normalization factor that was applied to the actual CPU consumption and converted the value back to seconds. Finally, we kept the jobs that start before (resp. end after) but end (resp. begin) within the considered period. This allows us to have a complete view of the workload over the 10 weeks. However, these jobs may be excluded for some of the specific analyses we present in the remaining of this section.

We developed a Python script to convert this information to the Standard Workload Format (SWF) [1] used by the Parallel Workloads Archive [3]. This format describes a job by 18 fields. While the conversion was straightforward for some of these fields, e.g., job number, submission, start, end and wait times, or number of allocated processors, others required more thinking and work.

The memory consumption of the jobs is logged by ARCo as two complementary metrics: the integral memory usage expressed in GB.CPU.seconds, i.e., the average memory consumption of the job, and the *maximum Resident Set Size* (RSS). We decided to keep the latter as exceeding the maximum amount of memory allowed by the configuration of a queue would cause the failure of the job. Consequently, we also used the RSS as the requested amount of memory, even though jobs also expressed requirements related to Virtual Memory.

The most problematic field in this conversion to the SWF format was the *time requested* by jobs. Indeed, the run time of a job is classically computed as the difference between its end and start times. However, at submission time, users are encouraged to express their requests not as a hard or soft walltime limit (using the h_rt or s_rt flags) but as a hard or soft CPU time limit (using the h_cpu or s_cpu flags). Again, this is dictated by the pledging and accounting procedures that use HS06 as main metric, and thus an efficient CPU consumption as both an objective and a performance indicator. To reflect this peculiar way of expressing the maximal duration of a job, we fill the *Requested Time* field of the SWF with the *CPU Time* requested by users.

Information about users and groups has been anonymized by converting them to integer values. The configuration of UGE allows administrators to distinguish different *projects* within a user group. For instance, for the ATLAS collaboration, the Monte-Carlo simulation jobs do not belong to the same project as the data analysis jobs. As the induced workloads may differ a lot from one project to another within a single user group, we decided to reflect this differences in the produced SWF file by using the *project* information rather than the *group* one.

For the fields related to the queue and partition to which a job has been scheduled, we associate two conversion tables to the SWF logs. There are six queues, described in Table 2, and two partitions defined by the running Operating System, whose boundaries evolved over the considered period as shown in Fig. 1. Finally, three fields (i.e., *Executable (Application) Number*, *Preceding Job Number*, and *Think Time from Preceding Job*) remain undefined as the corresponding information was not logged by UGE.

The resulting SWF file is composed of 7,607,154 individual jobs. Almost 90% of these jobs (i.e., 6,824,118 jobs) are sequential. However, if we consider the cumulative CPU consumption of jobs, we observe a different distribution. Multi-core jobs represent about 40% of the CPU consumption. More precisely, 96.1% of these multi-core jobs run on eight cores and are submitted by only two users groups: ATLAS (73.3%) and CMS (22.8%).

We start our analysis by comparing the CPU usage made by the different user groups to their pledges. This is a way to measure how well the job scheduler allocates resources to groups with the objective of respecting the fair-share that derives from these pledges. Figure 3a shows the observed distribution of the CPU usage over 10 weeks while Fig. 3b shows how the pledges for computing power were distributed among the different user groups for 2018. We only distinguish the groups whose shares are greater than 2% of the total CPU consumption in these graphs for the sake of readability. The "Other Experiments" section aggregates the usages and pledges of the more than 70 other user groups.

The fact that most of the user groups with the largest pledges are also the biggest consumers of CPU resources confirms the overall respect of the fair-share by the batch scheduling system. On both graphs, the four LHC experiments (ATLAS, CMS, Alice, and LHCb) have the biggest shares, which explains why the whole resource allocation procedure and the performance objectives assigned to the job scheduler are driven by the demands of these groups. However, those graphs also show large discrepancies between pledges and usages that can be explained by the combination of several factors. First, the submission patterns of the different groups vary over the year in periods of high or low activity. Another monitoring tool used by the operation team shows that the two groups that are among the top pledgers but not among the top users (i.e., CTA and HESS) did not submit enough jobs to meet their objectives for the second quarter of the year. Conversely, the Alice, CMS, and LHCb groups increased their submissions with regard to their objectives and took advantage of these unused

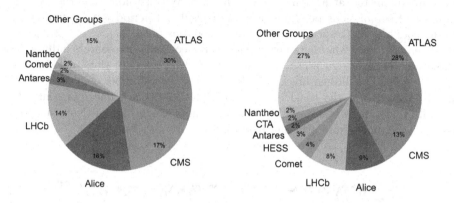

**Fig. 3.** Distribution of the computing resource consumptions (a) and requests (b) among the different scientific collaborations using the CC-IN2P3.

shares. Second, the upgrade of the default OS and the moving boundaries of the partitions shown by Fig. 1 were beneficial to some groups that were among the first to migrate. They were thus able to access a less crowded set of nodes while others groups had to compete for a smaller amount of CPU resources. However, we consider that this behavior is related to a transient yet impacting event and should not have appeared so clearly with a single stable partition.

An important characteristic of the considered workload is that almost half the jobs (47.55% or 3,615,225 jobs) are submitted through a *grid middleware stack* while the other half (52.45% or 3,991,929 jobs) is submitted by actual users directly to the batch systems. Figure 4 shows the *daily* (left) and *weekly* (right) arrival rates for these *Grid* and *Batch* jobs.

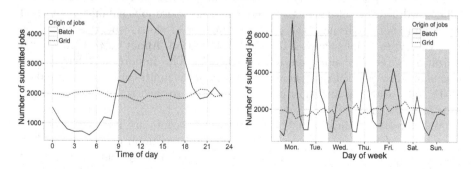

**Fig. 4.** Daily (left) and weekly (right) arrival rates for Grid and Batch jobs. For the daily arrival rate, the gray area depicts the typical working hours.

We clearly observe two different submission patterns. While the batch job arrival rate follows a traditional "working hours and business days" pattern, grid jobs are submitted at an almost constant rate. We also note that the average number of submissions per hour over the considered period is very similar for both types of jobs (respectively 1956 and 2160 jobs per hour).

Then, we study what is the utilization of the computing resources induced by these submissions. Figure 5 shows how many virtual cores (or slots) are simultaneously used. The dashed black line indicates the total number of available slots which evolved over the considered period. The solid black line represents the overall utilization, while the other two lines show which part of this utilization respectively comes from grid and batch jobs.

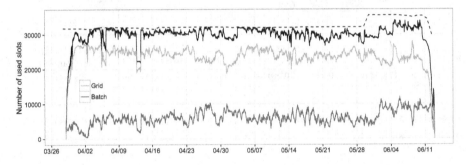

**Fig. 5.** Utilization of the resources, in terms of slots, over the considered period. The dashed black line indicates the total number of available slots, the solid black line represents the overall utilization and the other two lines show which part of this utilization respectively comes from grid and batch jobs.

We observe that one of the major operational objectives of the CC-IN2P3 is met as the utilization is generally well over 90%. One noticeable exception is around April 13th when a change in the configuration of UGE prevented jobs to be scheduled. We also see that while there are more jobs submitted by local users than coming through the grid, the number of slots respectively used by these two types of jobs shows a different distribution. About 80% of the overall utilization in terms of slots comes from grid jobs. This important difference can be explained by the fact that the vast majority of the multi-core jobs executed on CC-IN2P3's resources and most of the jobs related to the four LHC experiments come from the grid.

An interesting thing to note is that when less slots are used by grid jobs, more are used by batch jobs to reach a close to maximum overall utilization. This could mean that the jobs and resource management system makes a good job at balancing the resource allocations between the two categories of jobs. However, if we consider the number of pending slot requests, i.e., the sum of the numbers of slots requested by jobs waiting in the queues, we observe a less ideal situation shown by Fig. 6.

We observe that there are much less pending requests for grid jobs than for batch jobs. Over the whole period, around 3,000 slots are requested by grid jobs that have to wait for resources to be available while this average is of nearly 14,000 for batch jobs. The difference between the maximum number of pending slot requests is even more glaring: 7,400 for grid jobs and 79,200 for batch jobs. More importantly, we observe three periods (April 16–20, May 3–4, and June 4–7) where this number of pending slot requests for batch jobs remains well above 15,000 for more than two days.

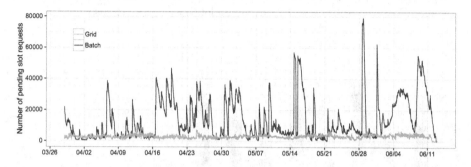

**Fig. 6.** Evolution of the number of pending slot requests over the considered period with regard to the job category.

Several factors can explain the results shown in Fig. 6. First, the differences in submission patterns illustrated in Fig. 4 indicate that a high number of batch jobs can be submitted at certain periods and needs to be absorbed by the system. To some extent, we can observe peaks in Fig. 6 at the beginning of each week that match the higher submission rates for Mondays and Tuesday shown by Fig. 4 (right). Conversely, the almost constant submission rate of grid jobs can be straightforwardly translated in an almost constant number of slot requests and explain the little variations we observe for this category of jobs. Second, grid jobs are usually not directly submitted to the batch system. The middleware stacks used by the different experiments typically include another layer that control the submission rate according to the observed status of the queue and the number of running jobs. A third potential cause is that grid jobs are submitted by groups with the largest shares, hence the highest priorities. Then, batch jobs submitted by smaller groups tend to have lower priorities, experience more delays in their scheduling, and thus tend to accumulate in the scheduling queues. However, these reasons do not fully explain why the observed peaks in the number of pending slot requests take so much time to be absorbed by the system. To understand that, we have to look at the duration of the jobs.

Figure 7 shows the distribution of job duration and distinguishes grid jobs from batch jobs. In the studied log, 84% of the submitted jobs are in the `long` or `mc_long` queues whose limits are set to two days of CPU time. 4% are "long lasting" jobs that can consume for up to 7 days of CPU time, while the remaining 12% correspond to "huge" jobs which are limited to three days of CPU time.

As nearly 58% of the studied workload is composed of jobs that run for less than an hour, we created more intervals for these very short jobs. We observe two major peaks at more than 600,000 jobs in the less than a minute interval for batch jobs and in the five to fifteen minutes for grid jobs. For grid jobs, the explanation of this large amount of very short jobs pertains to the use of *pilot jobs* to create a steady resource pool. When a pilot starts but realizes that it has no jobs to execute, it ends itself after a short time, i.e., up to 15 min. For batch jobs, failed jobs accounts for nearly 30% of the jobs that end in less than a minute. Other potential causes need to be investigated but the bulk of these very short jobs was submitted by only five identified users groups.

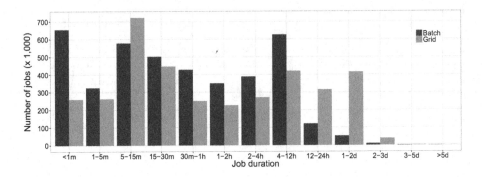

**Fig. 7.** Distribution of the number of jobs according to their run time from March 29, 2018 to June 12, 2018.

At the other end of the range of job duration, we can see that about 52,000 jobs (0.67%) have a duration greater than two days, which is the upper bound of the `long` queue. However, more than 41,000 of these jobs were submitted in the `long` queue. The reason is that these jobs do not fully use the CPU and can then run beyond the limit of 48 h of CPU time up to 58 h, which is the upper bound of this queue with regard to execution time. However, the vast majority of the jobs that were submitted to the `huge` and `longlasting` queues last for less than a day. This indicates that groups with an access to these reserved queues submitted jobs that should have gone in the regular `long` queue.

This analysis pleads for a redefinition of the scheduling queues, and the pools of resources they can access to better take the characteristics of the workload into account. For instance, a classical rule is to assign to a queue a number of resources that is inversely proportional to the duration of the jobs submitted in this queue [7]. The rationale is that the system can afford to concurrently execute a large number of short jobs, as they will release the resources soon. Conversely, the number of long running jobs has to be controlled to prevent large delays for shorter jobs caused by the lack of available resources. The importance of the configuration of the queues on the quality of the produced schedules has been outlined in [6,7]. However, such a work still has to be done at CC-IN2P3 and will require to measure and balance the effects of adding more queues to the system with regard to the respect of the fair sharing of the resources, hence the respect of the pledges made by the user groups. Having a precise estimation of the duration of a job at submission time is key to the success of such a redefinition of the scheduling queues.

Figure 8 shows that the estimations of the CPU time consumption associated to the jobs, when specified, are far from accurate. For batch jobs, many different estimations are provided by users, most of them being either straightforward (e.g., 12, 24, or 48 h) or arbitrary (e.g., 20,000 s or 47 h) values. For grid jobs the situation is even worse. The small set soft of CPU time requests shown by the steps in the grey line of the right panel of Fig. 8 are automatically added by one component of the grid middleware stack and correspond to the limits of the queues. These requests are thus not related to the profiles of the jobs at all. Improving these estimations will imply to better tune the configuration of the grid middleware component and to better inform and form the users about the consequences of the provided estimations on the scheduling of their jobs.

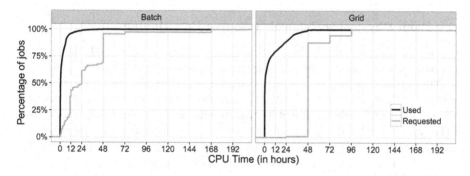

**Fig. 8.** Cumulative distribution functions (CDF) of actual and estimated job CPU times for batch and grid jobs.

We end this characterization of this 10-week workload executed at CC-IN2P3 by considering the distribution of the CPU utilization with regard to the duration of the jobs. Figure 9 shows that jobs running in less than 24 h represent an important part of the system utilization which is not reflected in the configuration of queues. This also confirms the impact of multi-core jobs which only account for 10% of the submissions but 40% of the CPU consumption.

## 3   Reducing the Human-in-the-Loop Component

In this section, we motivate and explain the modifications made to the configuration of the job and resource management system during the year 2017. However, this experience report does not include any quantification of the benefits of these modifications. The main objective was to reduce the burden put on operators by

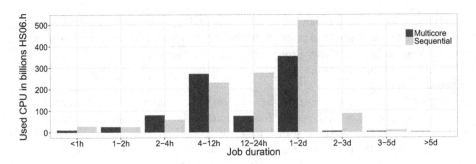

**Fig. 9.** Distribution of the CPU usage by job run time.

improving the decisions made by the batch scheduling system, hence automating some of their daily interventions. Such interventions were not tracked before the modifications. The evaluation of the gain would thus have been subjective and difficult to quantify.

### 3.1 From Physical to Logical Resource Partitioning

Despite the efforts made while purchasing new hardware to keep the computing infrastructure as homogeneous as possible, nodes used to differ a lot in terms of CPU power and amount of memory from one model to another. A direct consequence of this heterogeneity was that some nodes were more suited than others to the execution of the 8-core jobs that require more memory. As mentioned in the previous section, almost all of these jobs are submitted by the two main experiments (in terms of resource allocation and consumption) running at the CC-IN2P3. They are thus considered of the highest priority.

Before March 2017, the computing infrastructure was physically partitioned in three *host groups* as shown in Fig. 10. One was dedicated to sequential jobs (125 nodes), another to multi-core jobs (245 nodes), and the third and largest one (330 nodes) accepted the execution of both sequential and multi-core jobs.

The primary motivation of such a partitioning was to guarantee that the high priority multi-core jobs can start without having to wait for the completion of several sequential jobs. A secondary motivation was to keep the capacity to allow sequential jobs to run on these nodes dedicated to multi-core jobs when they become idle. The major physics collaborations such as ATLAS or CMS usually execute an important part of their computations during planned *campaigns*. They are also able to coordinate the use of multiple computing centers at a continental scale to distribute the load. Then, there can be variations in the job submission pattern, and periods of lower load could be exploited by other user groups. However, this management of distinct resource pools had a high operational cost. For instance, if a decrease in the submission of multi-core jobs by the ATLAS experiment was detected by the operators, they first had to check with the dedicated support to determine if this behavior was expected and know the duration of the lower load period. Then, nodes were manually reassigned

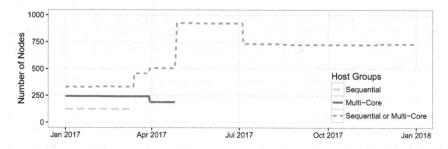

**Fig. 10.** Transition from a physical to a logical node partitioning in 2017. The variation of the number of nodes from May to July corresponds to the period between the reception of new nodes and the decommission of old hardware.

to the mutualized host group to keep them utilized. A safety margin was kept in case the submission rate of ATLAS starts to increase earlier than excepted. This safety margin could be exploited by other groups running multi-core jobs such as CMS, but as the estimated end of the low load period got closer, more stringent limitations had to be manually applied to these groups.

With the end of Moore's Law, the node heterogeneity tends to disappear. New processors have more cores but there are no important clock rate deltas from one generation to another anymore. The historical physical partitioning of the resources is thus no longer justified. To simplify the management of the computing infrastructure, it has been replaced by a logical partitioning. In other words, the existing host groups have been merged, as shown by Fig. 10, and the distinction between sequential and multi-core jobs is now handled by the queues presented in Table 2. This change is almost transparent for the users (who are not supposed to specify a queue) as the job scheduler can automatically assign multi-core jobs to one of the mc_* queues. However, this is an important change from the operational point of view. Indeed, operators no longer have to manually specify the boundaries of the resource pools based on experience and rough estimations of the foreseen evolution of the submission patterns. This burden is now transferred to the job scheduling system which has been designed to adapt its decisions according to the respective filling of the queues.

## 3.2   Simplification of the Access Rule and Quota Mechanisms

The origin of the definition of *resources* and the application of quotas on these resources goes back to the use of the BQS job and resource management system. The term "resource" first encompassed job related parameters such as the required operating system, the needed amount of memory, the maximum CPU time, or the queue in which to place the job. This definition was rapidly extended to cover the different services offered by the CC-IN2P3 that a job could need.

A motivating example for such a definition of resources and quotas is the case of a job that need to fetch data from a distributed storage system $S_1$, store the produced results on another storage system $S_2$, and also needs to access a relational database $D$ during its execution. Such a job can succeed if and only if all of the three dependencies on external services $S_1$, $S_2$, and $D$ can be satisfied. Specifying the needed resources at submission time allows the job scheduler to delay a job if one or more services are not available (e.g., because of an incident or a temporary saturation) to prevent an unavoidable failure of the job.

This mechanism has then evolved into a two-level quota mechanism. The first level defines global limits on the number of concurrent jobs that can access a given resource without regard to the submitter. Such limits allow to prevent the different storage subsystems or database services to be overloaded, ensure that the number of license tokens for a commercial software is not exceeded, or define physical pools with different versions of the operating system when an upgrade in underway. The second level specifies quotas for {resource, group} couples. The rationale is to be able to block or limit the access of a given group to a specific service more easily. For instance, if a group has filled its allocated disk space on a storage subsystem, jobs that could write more data will be rejected until more space has been granted or cleaning has been made. This also allows operators to easily drain the use of a resource for maintenance operations or incident recovery by blocking all the jobs that expressed a dependency on that resource.

Over the years, this appealing way to ensure a fine regulation of the job submission and to optimize the utilization of the computing and storage infrastructures became a very complex set of rules, thresholds, and locks to control the maximum number of jobs per user, group, machine, or service. The multiplication of resource definitions, hence the accumulation of limits for a given user group not only slows down the scheduling rounds as the job scheduler has to check everything, but also makes it sometimes difficult to understand why some jobs cannot enter the system. For instance, a restrictive limit may have been applied at some point, and for a good reason, to a certain {resource, group} couple and not been reconsidered afterwards. Then, sometimes months later, users complain that their jobs do not run for what they consider as no good reason, because of this persisting but forgotten limit.

At the end of 2016 the decision has been made to simplify the access rule and quota mechanisms. The main objective was to reduce the number of declared *resources* to only keep a minimal set of essential requirements that jobs have to express. The CC-IN2P3 being a production center, such changes have to be done carefully to prevent any major disruption of the activity. The chosen solution was to progressively relax the quota associated to a {resource, group} when it becomes a bottleneck while ensuring that the associated resource can cope with the increase. Figure 11 illustrates this action. Eventually, when the limit is high enough, it obviously becomes meaningless and can thus be safely removed. This was especially done for quotas related to the storage subsystem.

A similar method has been applied to the maximum number of jobs of a group that can run simultaneously. Such RQS were defined as a way to enforce the fair-share and to be able to rapidly react to an unwanted overconsumption of the resources by a given group. However, this kind of limit was especially harmful to small user groups whose computing needs correspond to short bursts

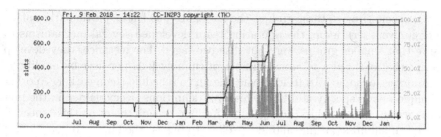

**Fig. 11.** Relaxation of a per-group RQS on a storage subsystem. The black line indicates the maximum number of *slots* (i.e., virtual cores) currently available to the group. The grey part corresponds to the number of used slots.

of a large number of jobs every once in a while, for instance just before a deadline for the submission of an article. In such a case, users had to open an issue on the user support ticketing system to explain that they would like to see more of their jobs running. Then, the operation team would grant this exception by manually relaxing the quota and/or boosting the priority of jobs.

After a few months of operation, we can conclude that letting the job scheduler deal with submission bursts without any human intervention is a success. The concerned groups reduced their time to solution without harming other groups. This also reduces the load of both the operation and support teams who have less tickets to handle. However, some limits have to be kept for certain groups whose jobs have a specific greedy behavior or are highly sensitive to the accessibility of the storage subsystems.

### 3.3   Extending the Fair-Share History Window

The last important modification made to the configuration of the job scheduler is related to the implementation of the fair sharing of resources. The basic principle of a fair-share allocation is, for each user/group, to assign a priority to jobs that is inversely proportional to the usage of the resources by this user/group over a sliding time frame. The rationale is very simple: if a group already computed a lot, it has to make room for another that did not. Then, this group will compute less (and see its priority increase) while the other computes more (and its priority decreases). A key configuration parameter of such an algorithm is the size of the time frame over which to compute the resource usage.

Until the end of 2016, the size of this history window was set to 24 h. As for many other parameters, this value was motivated by the predominance of the LHC-related jobs in the workload and the commitment to fulfill the pledges for these experiments made by the CC-IN2P3. Such a short time window was one of the levers to ensure a good reactivity of the system when the largest groups, i.e., ATLAS or CMS, started to submit jobs after a period of inactivity. These jobs got the highest possible priority and were scheduled immediately.

The main drawback of this strategy is that the jobs submitted by groups with much lower priorities suffered from large delays. From the point of view of the users belonging to these groups, the fair-share was felt as particularly unfair. To circumvent this issue, the operation team developed several mechanisms to ensure that smaller groups were not disadvantaged. For instance, they develop a script that ensured a minimal number of running jobs per user by modifying the priorities of some jobs to force the system to schedule them earlier. Another technique was to specify additional resource definitions (as explained in the previous section) dedicated to these groups. Adding a requirement on this "special" resource at submission time allowed the jobs to bypass the fair-share mechanism completely and start almost immediately.

The proposed solution to ensure a fair sharing of the resources for *all* the user groups, be they small or big consumers, without having to bypass or modify the decisions made by the job scheduler was to increase the time frame used to determine the priorities. To prevent any harmful disruption of the production due to this change, we decided to progressively and empirically increase this value. It was first set to 15 days in January 2017, then to 30 days in March, and finally to 90 days in June 2017. After each modification, the operation team monitored its impact on the production. While benefits for small groups and no loss of the quality of service for the largest groups were observed, the time frame was increased. A more principled process based on the particular setting of the CC-IN2P3 would obviously have to be found. However, this would require a parametric impact study combined to a thorough evaluation through simulation before being deployed in production that is part of our future work.

The second modification made to the priority determination mechanism is related to the metric used to measure the resource utilization. Historically, the priorities were based on the *used CPU time* because the pledges made by the experiments are expressed as a CPU consumption. This metric is thus used to determine if the computing infrastructure can satisfy all the pledges and for the accounting of the resource usage. However, it may also favor inefficient jobs, i.e., jobs that are unable to fully exploit the CPU. Let's consider two groups that submit one job of the same duration each, one using 100% of the CPU capacity and the other only 50%. Because of the chosen metric, the latter is seen as consuming less resources than the former over the same time period and will end up with a higher priority. Then the subsequent inefficient jobs from the second group will be scheduled earlier even though they "waste" CPU time.

The historical way to address this issue was to add a new quota to limit the number of inefficient jobs running, hence adding more complexity to the scheduling. A simpler solution, adopted in September 2017, was to change the metric from *used CPU time* to *actual run time*. This simple modification solved the issue of inefficient jobs without adding an extra complexity to the system. For the other jobs the change is transparent.

## 4    Conclusion and Future Work

The IN2P3 Computing Center is the largest French academic High Throughput Computing center. Its primary mission is to answer the computing and storage needs of the major international scientific collaborations in the domains of high-energy and astroparticle physics. To manage the execution of millions of individual jobs every month on nearly 35,000 cores, the CC-IN2P3 relied for years on an in-house batch scheduling system, a complex set of admission rules, and quotas on hardware and software resources. However, the ever increasing sizes of both the infrastructure and workload made the existing system too cumbersome to maintain and put a heavy load on the operation team.

In this experience report, we presented the specificity of the CC-IN2P3, characterized the large HTC workload executed on its resources, and show how complex its operation has become. Then we detailed the work engaged at the end of 2016 to transfer some of the actions done by operators to the job scheduling system with the objective to minimize the "human-in-the-loop" component in scheduling decisions. The proposed modifications that were recently implemented shows preliminary but promising results. However, the work presented in this paper is only the beginning of a long-term activity to change the operation procedures applied to the computing infrastructure of the CC-IN2P3.

Our future work thus includes several directions that we plan to follow. First, we will continue the analysis of the workload to further characterize the jobs and identify leads for improvement. One of the main objective will be to work on a better estimation of the execution time of the jobs. Ideally, we would like to encourage users to provide better estimations of the walltime at submission time as it is classically done on HPC systems. This should both help the job and resource management system to schedule jobs and the operation team to refine the definition of queues. Second, we plan to resort to simulation to assess the impact of potential modifications of the configurations of queues and quotas as proposed in [6,7]. Several tools are available to perform such a simulation study, like Alea [8] or Batsim [2]. The main obstacle is that the "Human-in-the-loop" component that we started to reduce makes it difficult to use logs obtained from the job scheduler and replay them under a different configuration. Indeed, the scheduling decisions taken solely by the job and resource management system may have been altered by operators, without being reflected in the logs. This may lead to interpretation biases. Further reducing these human interventions is thus an essential step in the optimization of the configuration of the job scheduling system. Third, we plan to gather user feedback in a few months to measure the impact of the proposed modifications as perceived by the users. This will give us a complementary point of view on the benefits of this work and may outline new and unforeseen modifications to make. Finally, we would like to give access to contextualized logs to the job scheduling research community. As mentioned before, this requires more work to reduce the human interventions and to be able to indicate in the logs when operators modified the decisions taken by the system. We believe that the large HTC workload processed at the CC-IN2P3 has specific characteristics, detailed in Sect. 2.3 which are very different of what can be found in the Parallel Workloads Archive for instance. This will constitute a new source of interesting problems to solve for the research community, whose feedback would benefit to the operation of the CC-IN2P3.

**Acknowledgements.** The authors would like to thank the members of the Operation and Applications teams of the CC-IN2P3 for their help in the preparation of this experience report.

# References

1. Chapin, S.J., et al.: Benchmarks and standards for the evaluation of parallel job schedulers. In: Feitelson, D.G., Rudolph, L. (eds.) JSSPP 1999. LNCS, vol. 1659, pp. 67–90. Springer, Heidelberg (1999). https://doi.org/10.1007/3-540-47954-6_4
2. Dutot, P.-F., Mercier, M., Poquet, M., Richard, O.: Batsim: a realistic language-independent resources and jobs management systems simulator. In: Desai, N., Cirne, W. (eds.) JSSPP 2015-2016. LNCS, vol. 10353, pp. 178–197. Springer, Cham (2017). https://doi.org/10.1007/978-3-319-61756-5_10
3. Feitelson, D., Tsafrir, D., Krakov, D.: Experience with using the parallel workloads archive. J. Parallel Distrib. Comput. **74**(10), 2967–2982 (2014)
4. Jackson, D., Snell, Q., Clement, M.: Core algorithms of the Maui scheduler. In: Feitelson, D.G., Rudolph, L. (eds.) JSSPP 2001. LNCS, vol. 2221, pp. 87–102. Springer, Heidelberg (2001). https://doi.org/10.1007/3-540-45540-X_6
5. Kay, J., Lauder, P.: A fair share scheduler. Commun. ACM **31**(1), 44–55 (1988)
6. Klusáček, D., Tóth, Š.: On interactions among scheduling policies: finding efficient queue setup using high-resolution simulations. In: Silva, F., Dutra, I., Santos Costa, V. (eds.) Euro-Par 2014. LNCS, vol. 8632, pp. 138–149. Springer, Cham (2014). https://doi.org/10.1007/978-3-319-09873-9_12
7. Klusáček, D., Tóth, Š., Podolníková, G.: Real-life experience with major reconfiguration of job scheduling system. In: Desai, N., Cirne, W. (eds.) JSSPP 2015-2016. LNCS, vol. 10353, pp. 83–101. Springer, Cham (2017). https://doi.org/10.1007/978-3-319-61756-5_5
8. Klusáček, D., Tóth, V., Podolníková, G.: Complex Job Scheduling Simulations with Alea 4. In: Proceedings of the 9th EAI International Conference on Simulation Tools and Techniques (Simutools 2016), pp. 124–129. ICST, Prague (2016)
9. Michelotto, M., et al.: A comparison of HEP code with SPEC 1 benchmarks on multi-core worker nodes. J. Phys. Conf. Ser. **219**(5), 052009 (2010)
10. The ATLAS Collaboration: Observation of a new particle in the search for the standard model Higgs Boson with the ATLAS detector at the LHC. Phys. Lett. B **716**(1), 1–29 (2012). https://doi.org/10.1016/j.physletb.2012.08.020
11. The CMS Collaboration: Observation of a New Boson at a Mass of 125 GeV with the CMS experiment at the LHC. Phys. Lett. B **716**(1), 30–61 (2012). https://doi.org/10.1016/j.physletb.2012.08.021
12. The IN2P3/CNRS Computing Center. http://cc.in2p3.fr/en/
13. The LIGO Scientific Collaboration and Virgo Collaboration: Observation of gravitational waves from a binary black hole merger. Phys. Rev. Lett. **116**, 061102 (2016). https://doi.org/10.1103/PhysRevLett.116.061102
14. Univa Corporation: Grid Engine. http://www.univa.com/products/

# Using Pilot Systems to Execute Many Task Workloads on Supercomputers

Andre Merzky[1], Matteo Turilli[1], Manuel Maldonado[1], Mark Santcroos[1], and Shantenu Jha[1,2(✉)]

[1] RADICAL Laboratory, Electrical and Computer Engineering, Rutgers University, Piscataway, NJ, USA
shantenu.jha@rutgers.edu
[2] Brookhaven National Laboratory, Upton, NY, USA

**Abstract.** High performance computing systems have historically been designed to support applications comprised of mostly monolithic, single-job workloads. Pilot systems decouple workload specification, resource selection, and task execution via job placeholders and late-binding. Pilot systems help to satisfy the resource requirements of workloads comprised of multiple tasks. RADICAL-Pilot (RP) is a modular and extensible Python-based pilot system. In this paper we describe RP's design, architecture and implementation, and characterize its performance. RP is capable of spawning more than 100 tasks/second and supports the steady-state execution of up to 16K concurrent tasks. RP can be used stand-alone, as well as integrated with other application-level tools as a runtime system.

**Keywords:** Pilot system · Placeholder job · Multilevel scheduling
HPC workflow

## 1 Introduction

Traditionally, advances in high-performance scientific computing have focused on the scale, performance and optimization of a workload with a large but single task, and less on workloads comprised of multiple tasks. High-performance workflows and scalable computation of ensemble workloads are becoming increasingly important and are highly relevant to exploit post-Moore parallelism. As a result, the number and type of applications that can be formulated as workflows or ensembles is vast and span many scientific domains.

Applications with workloads comprised of multiple tasks impose sophisticated execution and advanced resource management requirements [1]. High-performance computing (HPC) systems have been designed to support applications comprised of mostly monolithic, single-job workloads. For example, HPC systems have been designed and operated to maximize overall system utilization, which typically entails static resource partitioning across jobs and users. Thus, there is a tension between the resource requirements of workloads comprised of

ⓒ Springer Nature Switzerland AG 2019
D. Klusáček et al. (Eds.): JSSPP 2018, LNCS 11332, pp. 61–82, 2019.
https://doi.org/10.1007/978-3-030-10632-4_4

many tasks, and the capabilities of the traditional HPC resource management as well as their usage policies. This tension motivates middleware that can efficiently manage the ability to support the resource requirements of many task workloads without compromising traditional capabilities of HPC systems.

Enter pilot systems. The authors in Ref. [2] defined the properties of the Pilot paradigm, and its relevance in the execution of workloads comprised of multiple tasks. A defining element of the Pilot paradigm is the execution of a workload via multi-entity and multi-stage scheduling on resource placeholders. Systems implementing the Pilot paradigm submit job placeholders (i.e., pilots) to the scheduler of resources. Once active, each pilot accepts and executes tasks directly submitted to it by the application. In this way, pilot systems decouple workload specification, resource selection, and task execution via job placeholders and late-binding.

Pilot systems address two apparently contradictory requirements: accessing HPC resources via their centralized schedulers, and letting applications independently schedule tasks on the acquired portion of resources. Thus, pilot systems provide a simple solution to the rigid resource management model historically found in HPC systems. Not surprisingly, many workflow management systems use pilot systems. Surprisingly, in spite of the acceptance and uptake of pilot systems, to the best of our knowledge, there are no general purpose implementations capable of working in production with multiple HPC resources, including leadership class machines.

In this paper, we discuss the design, architecture and implementation of RADICAL-Pilot (RP) (Sect. 3). RP is a pilot system that fully implements the concepts and capabilities of the Pilot paradigm. The implementation of RP differs from other pilot systems mostly in terms of API, portability, and introspection. Implemented in Python, RP is a self-contained pilot system which can be used to provide a runtime system for workloads comprised of multiple tasks. In Sect. 4, we discuss how RP provides pilot capabilities on Cray systems such as *Blue Waters* and *Titan*. We experimentally characterize RP at multiple levels in Sect. 5: we study the performance of individual components of RP, followed by the integrated performance of its Agent. We then investigate the resource utilization and performance of both the native and enhanced scheduling algorithms.

The absolute performance of the enhanced scheduler is less important than the ability to enhance performance of the scheduler via extensions and customized scheduling algorithms. This reiterates the core contribution of this paper: a careful description of the design and implementation of RP, highlighting its use of multi-level and multi-entity scheduling.

## 2    Related Work

Traditionally, HPC systems such as Crays have been designed to best support monolithic workloads. However, the workload of many important scientific applications is constructed out of spatially and temporally heterogeneous tasks that are often dynamically inter-related, where those tasks require compute, memory and communication capabilities exceeding what single node machine can provide, and where the *overall* workload requirements are comparable to or exceeding those of classic HPC workloads [3–5]. These workloads can benefit from being executed at scale on supercomputers (e.g., *Blue Waters* and *Titan*, both Cray systems), but a tension exists among the workloads' resource utilization requirements like rapidly and repeatedly acquiring a certain amount of cores over time, the capabilities of the HPC system software, and their usage policies. Pilot systems have the potential to relieve this tension but their adoption for this class of HPC systems present several challenges that, so far, have not been fully addressed.

Since 1995, more than twenty pilot systems have been developed [2]. Most of these systems are tailored to specific workloads, resources, interfaces, or development models. Most pilot systems have been implemented to optimize the throughput of single-core (or single-node), short-lived, uncoupled tasks [2]. Some notable examples are: HTCondor with Glidein on OSG [6], one of the most widely used pilot systems for the execution of mostly single-core workloads; the pilot systems developed for the LHC communities which execute millions of jobs a week [7] and are specialized in supporting LHC workloads on specific resources like those of WLCG; the light-weight execution framework called Falkon, which represents an early stand-alone pilot system for HPC environment [8]; and Coasters, developed mostly to support the Swift workflow system [9].

One of the major challenges in developing a general-purpose pilot system, capable of executing multi-task workloads on supercomputers, is supporting multiple task launch methods, each with a specific set of limitations. For example, Cluster Compatibility Mode (CCM) [10] is designed to provide services analogous to those of Beowulf clusters but is not generally available on all Cray installations and, when present, access to it varies per system. The Application Level Placement Scheduler (ALPS) [11] system, provides launch functionality for running executables on compute nodes but limits the number of concurrent applications a user can run by default. The Open Run-Time Environment [12], a component of the OpenMPI MPI implementation, supports distributed high-performance computing applications operating in a heterogeneous environment but the degree of adoption and support varies across Cray systems.

Tools have been developed to support spatially and/or temporally heterogeneous tasks on Crays but many of these tools are built on top of CCM, ALPS, or use single MPI allocations. As such, they are not able to support task heterogeneity or reach the necessary level of execution concurrency. For example, TaskFarmer [13], a tool developed at LBNL, enables the user to execute a list of system commands from a task file, allowing single-core or single-node tasks to be run within a single `mpirun` allocation. Wraprun [14], a utility developed at ORNL, enables independent execution of multiple MPI applications under a single `aprun` call. QDO [15], a lightweight high-throughput queuing system for workflows that have many small tasks has to use the resource batch system for job submission. MySGE [16], another tool developed at LBNL that allows users to create a private Sun GridEngine cluster on large parallel systems, but is only available on NERSC resources. Python Task Farm (PTF) [17], a utility for running serial Python programs as multiple independent copies of a program over many cores, is available only on ARCHER (at EPCC).

The Pilot paradigm has proven sufficiently useful that resource management systems have begun to include pilot capabilities either as separate tooling, or as part of their implementation. For example, Flux [18] is described as a next-generation Scalable Resource and Job Management Software (RJMS) for HPC centers that focuses on a new paradigm of resource and job management. Within this new paradigm, Flux allows resource allocation to be dynamic (i.e., dynamic workloads), a key design principle of the Pilot paradigm [2]. This results in jobs having the ability to scale up to a maximum requested resources (e.g., CPU cores, GPUs, etc.) during execution, or to execute workloads (i.e., workloads with different resource requirements) on a single "dynamic" allocation. Unfortunately, Flux is limited only to the HPC resources that use it as their RJMS. Further, as of the writing of this paper, Flux is still on an Alpha release.

## 3   RADICAL-Pilot

RADICAL-Pilot (RP) is a scalable and interoperable pilot system that implements the Pilot abstraction to support the execution of diverse workloads. We describe the design and architecture of RP, and characterize the performance of RP's task execution components. These components are engineered for efficient resource utilization while maintaining the full generality of the Pilot abstraction. RP supports several Cray machines, including *Blue Waters* (NCSA), *Titan* (ORNL), and ARCHER (EPSRC), and a whole range of other platforms.

### 3.1   Overall Architecture

RP is a runtime system designed to execute heterogeneous and dynamic workloads on multiple and diverse resources. RP's architecture and execution model are shown in Fig. 1: workloads and pilots are described via the Pilot-API and passed *(1)* to the RP runtime system, which submits the pilots, launches the pilots' Agent, and executes the tasks of the workload on one or more Agents. RP represents pilots as aggregates of resources, independent from the architecture and topology of the target machines, and workloads as a set of units to be executed on the resources of the pilot. Both pilots and units are stateful entities, each with a well-defined state model and life cycle. Their states and state transitions are managed via the three modules of the RP architecture: PilotManager, UnitManager, and Agent.

The PilotManager submits pilots to resources via the RADICAL-SAGA API *(2)*. The SAGA API [19] implements an adapter for each type of supported resource, exposing uniform methods for job and data management. The Unit-Manager schedules units to pilots' Agent for execution. A MongoDB database is used to communicate the scheduled workload *(4)* between the UnitManager and

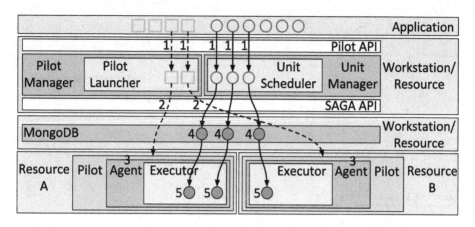

**Fig. 1.** RADICAL-Pilot Architecture and execution model.

one or more Agent. For this reason, the database instance needs to be accessible both from the user's workstation and the target resources, via ssh tunnels that RP creates at runtime, where needed and when possible. Each Agent bootstraps on a remote resource, pulls units from the MongoDB instance, and manages their execution on the cores held by the pilot *(5)*.

The modules of RP are distributed between the user workstation and the target resources. The PilotManager and UnitManager are executed on the user workstation while each Agent runs on the target resources. RP requires Linux or OS X with Python 2.7 on the workstation but the Agent can execute different types of units on resources with diverse architectures and software environments.

## 3.2 Programming Model

RP is engineered as a Python library that enables the declarative definition of resource requirements, and of workloads to execute on them. RP exposes a pilot-specific application programming interface called Pilot-API and enables programming of application-specific relationships between resources and workload in generic Python. In the following code snippets, we walk the reader through a minimal but complete example of running a workload on *Blue Waters* using RP.

```
# Create a session.
session = rp.Session()

# create a pilot manager.
pmgr = rp.PilotManager(session)

# create a unit manager.
umgr = rp.UnitManager(session)
```

**Fig. 2.** Pilot API. Declaration of Pilot-Manager and UnitManager within a session.

In Fig. 2, we show the code used to declare the respective managers for pilots and units, whose lifetime is managed by a session object. As such, closing a session destroys all its managers.

```
# Declare a 64-core pilot that will
# be available for 10 minutes.
pdesc = rp.ComputePilotDescription({
        'resource' : ncsa.bw,
        'cores'    : 64,
        'runtime'  : 10,
        'queue'    : 'debug',
        'project'  : 'gkd'
    })

# Submit the pilot for launching.
pilot = pmgr.submit_pilots(pdesc)

# Make the pilot resources available
# to a unit manager.
umgr.add_pilots(pilot)
```

(a)

```
# Number of units to run.
cuds = []
for i in range(0,42):
    # create a new CU description,
    # and fill it.
    cud = rp.ComputeUnitDescription()
    cud.executable = '/bin/date'
    cuds.append(cud)

# Submit units.
umgr.submit_units(cuds)

# Wait for the completion of units.
umgr.wait_units()

# Tear down pilots and managers.
session.close()
```

(b)

**Fig. 3.** Pilot API. **(a)** Declaration of a pilot, its subsequent submission to the Pilot-Manager and the association to a UnitManager. **(b)** Declaration and submission of compute units (CU).

In Fig. 3(a), we declare a pilot (`rp.ComputePilotDescription()`) by specifying the resource on which it should be instantiated, how many cores it should use, its runtime and, optionally, to what queue it should be submitted and to what project it should be charged. Once submitted via the PilotManager (`pmgr.submit_pilots()`), the pilot is asynchronously queued to the batch system of the indicated resource. Finally, the pilot is associated with a UnitManager (`umgr.add_pilots()`) to enable the execution of units on that pilot.

Finally, in Fig. 3(b) we declare a workload by creating a set of compute units (`cuds`) that specify what payload should be run (`/bin/date`). Once created, the compute units are submitted to the UnitManager (`umgr.submit_units()`) which schedules the unit to a pilot. The UnitManager can perform early binding (schedule to any known pilot) or late binding (delay scheduling until pilots become active). In either case, once that pilot does become active, it pulls the scheduled units for execution. The `umgr.wait_units()` call blocks until all the units have run to completion. Upon its return, the session is closed (`session.close()`) indicating that the workload execution has completed.

### 3.3   State and Execution Models

The lifespan of pilots has 4 states distributed among the PilotManager, resource, and pilot instance (Fig. 4a). Pilots are instantiated in the state NEW by the Pilot-Manager, wait in a queue to be launched, and transition to PM_LAUNCH when submitted to a Resource Manager (RM) via the SAGA API. Pilots wait in the queue of the RM and, once scheduled, become P_ACTIVE. They remain in this state until the end of their lifetime, when they transition to DONE.

The unit state model has 9 states distributed across the UnitManager, MongoDB instance, and Agent (Fig. 4b). Instantiated in the state NEW by the

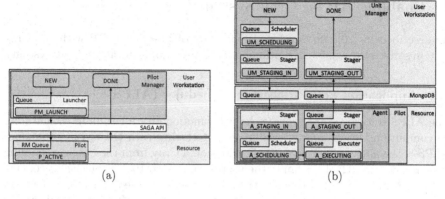

**Fig. 4.** (a) Architecture of RP Client and pilot state model. (b) Architecture of RP Agent and unit state model.

UnitManager, every unit is scheduled on an Agent (UM_SCHEDULING) via a queue on a MongoDB instance. The unit is then scheduled on the required number of cores held by the Agent's pilot (A_SCHEDULING), and finally executed (A_EXECUTING).

When required by a unit, input data are staged in by the UnitManager and Agent (UM_STAGING_IN, A_STAGING_IN), and output data are staged out (A_STAGING_OUT, U_STAGING_OUT) to a specified destination, e.g., local/shared filesystem or user workstation. Both input and output staging are optional, depending on the requirements of the units. The actual file transfers are enacted via local OS commands or RADICAL-SAGA, supporting (gsi)-scp, (gsi)-(s)ftp, and Globus Online.

The state transitions of Fig. 4 are sequential, and every transition can fail or be canceled by the PilotManager or UnitManager. All state transitions are managed by the PilotManager, UnitManager, and Agent components. The only special case is the transition of the pilots to the state P_ACTIVE which is determined by the resource's RM and managed by the PilotManager.

### 3.4 Agent Architecture

Depending on the resource architecture, the Agent's Stager, Scheduler, and Executer components (Fig. 4(b)) can be placed on cluster head nodes, machine oriented mini-server (MOM) nodes, compute nodes, virtual machines, or any combination thereof. Multiple Stager and Executer components can coexist in a single Agent, placed on any service node or compute node of the pilot's resource assignment. ZeroMQ communication bridges connect the Agent components, creating a network to support the transition of units through components. Every unit goes through the states of Input Staging, Scheduling, Execution & Output Staging. This paper investigates different implementations of launch methods, which are part of the Executer component, responsible for defining and managing the task execution process.

# 4  Enabling RP on Cray Systems

As described in [20], we developed four ways of interfacing RP with the Cray
system software to enable execution of distributed applications on Cray systems.

## 4.1  Application Level Placement Scheduler (ALPS)

The ALPS software suite provides launch functionality for running executables
on compute nodes of a Cray system, by interfacing with the aprun command.
ALPS is the native way to run applications on a Cray from the batch scheduling
system. By default, ALPS limits the user to run up to 1000 applications concurrently within one batch job but in the pilot use-case, these applications may run
only for a very short time. This strains ALPS and the MOM node, effectively
limiting the throughput of concurrent executions to around 100 applications.
Further, ALPS does not allow the user to easily run more than one task on a
single compute node, making it difficult, if not impossible, to run workloads with
tasks requiring single or small amount of cores and workloads with heterogeneous
task size.

## 4.2  Cluster Compatibility Mode (CCM)

Crays are massively parallel processing (MPP) machines and the Cray Compute Node OS does not provide the full set of Linux services typically found on
Beowulf clusters. CCM is a software suite designed to reduce this gap by providing services analogous to those of Beowulf clusters when required by applications. Nonetheless, CCM is not generally available on all Cray installations and,
when present, access to CCM varies per system, requiring special flags to the
job description or submitting to a special queue.

RP hides the CCM deployment differences from the application by operating the Agent either externally or internally to the CCM cluster created when
submitting a job to the Cray machine. When the Agent runs outside the CCM
cluster, it uses ccmrun to start tasks. However, this approach still relies on ALPS,
inheriting all the limitations described above. When the Agent runs within the
CCM cluster, only the initial startup of the Agent relies on ALPS. After that,
all task launching is done within the cluster, e.g., by using SSH or MPIRUN,
without further interaction with ALPS.

## 4.3  Open Run-Time Environment (OpenRTE/ORTE)

The Open Run-Time Environment is a spin-off from the Open-MPI project and
is a critical component of the OpenMPI MPI implementation. It was developed
to support distributed high-performance computing applications operating in a
heterogeneous environment. The system transparently provides support for inter-
process communication, resource discovery and allocation, and process launch
across a variety of platforms. ORTE provides a mechanism similar to the Pilot

concept—it allows the user to create a dynamic virtual machine (DVM) that spans multiple nodes. In regular OpenMPI usage the lifetime of the DVM is that of the application, but the DVM can also be made persistent, and we rely on this particular feature for RP. RP supports two different modes for interacting with the ORTE DVM: via orte-submit CLI calls, and via ORTE library calls. Currently we can not run applications that are linked against the Cray MPI libraries, but once Cray moves to PMIx [21] that issue is resolved.

Figure 5 shows the layout of the RP agent, the ORTE Head Node Process (HNP) that manages the DVM on the MOM Node, and the ORTE Daemons that run on the Compute Nodes.

**Command Line Interface (CLI):** Recently, ORTE has been extended with tools to expose the creation of the persistent DVM (orte-dvm) and the launching of tasks onto that DVM (orte-submit). The setup of the DVM requires a single ALPS interaction, after which all the tasks are executed independent of ALPS. As RP is a Python application and ORTE is implemented in C, we interface the two systems using the ORTE CLI. While this enabled concurrent task execution and sharing nodes among tasks, we did run into new bottlenecks. The interaction with the filesystem becomes a limiting factor for task execution as every task requires the execution of orte-submit. We also experience network socket race conditions and system resource limits above 16000 concurrent tasks, as every task requires an orte-submit instance that communicates independently with the orte-dvm. RP has the ability to spread the execution management of tasks over multiple compute nodes, addressing the problem of having a large centralized process footprint for maintaining state about each running process this way.

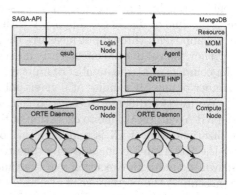

**Fig. 5.** Architecture overview of RP with ORTE backend.

**C Foreign Function Interface for Python (CFFI):** CFFI [22] provides a convenient and reliable way to call compiled C code from Python using interface declarations written in C. This mode of operation is similar to the CLI mode, but differs in the way RP interfaces with ORTE: RP launches each task using a library call instead of the orte-submit tool. This also allows the re-use of network socket, thus further decreasing the per-call overhead. The incentive for developing this approach was to overcome the limits and overheads imposed by the CLI approach. We called the resulting launch method "ORTE-LIB".

# 5  Experiments

We characterize the performance of the RP Agent by performing experiments to benchmark individual components and integrated experiments on the Agent as a whole. The results of experiments on individual components, referred to as microbenchmarks, characterize the performance of a component in isolation, while integrated experiments characterize the performance of a pipeline of components, taking into account the communication and coordination overheads of their orchestration. Experiments were performed on two Cray systems: *Blue Waters* at NCSA, and *Titan* at ORNL.

We use two metrics to characterize the performance of individual components: throughput and concurrency. As seen in Sect. 3, the RP Agent is designed as a pipeline of distinct components with multiple instances. For each instance of a component, throughput measures the rate at which units are managed, concurrency the volume of concurrently managed units. We measure the throughput of a component as the number of units it handles per second, concurrency as the number of units it handles at a given point in time.

We use two different metrics to characterize the integrated performance of the RP Agent: total time to execution of the given workload (TTX) and resource utilization (RU). TTX is a measure of how fast a set of tasks can be executed by the RP Agent. It includes the time taken by the RP Agent to manage and spawn the units for execution and the time taken by the units to execute. RU is a measure of the percentage of available core-time spent executing the workload and/or the RP Agent. TTX and RU are relevant for HPC resources, which traditionally have been designed to execute large parallel jobs and maximize overall utilization.

Depending on the type of experiment, the number of units, number or cores per unit, duration of the unit, number of instances of a component, and number of cores of a pilot are configurable parameters. By varying the values of these parameters, we measure the amount of units that are in a specific state as a function of time, or the time duration spent in a specific state. For example, we measure the number of units in state A_SCHEDULING and A_EXECUTING at every point in time in the RP Agent Scheduler component and derive the throughput of that component.

To capture all of the measurements mentioned above, RP is instrumented with a profiling facility to record timestamps of its operations. As the execution of a given workload proceeds (as described in Sect. 3.3), each state transition is recoded as an event. These events are written to disk for postmortem analysis via dedicated utility methods. RP's profiler is designed to be non-invasive and to have minimal effect on the runtime. We measured the temporal overhead of the profiler with a dedicated benchmark: For the same workload executed on the same resources, the overall running time of the Agent was $(144.7 \pm 19.2\,\mathrm{s})$ with profiling, and $(157.1 \pm 8.3\,\mathrm{s})$ without. Note how the standard deviation of the two measurements overlap, making the difference between the two execution times statistically insignificant.

The execution of workloads with multiple tasks on a pilot has a varying degree of concurrency, depending on the total number of cores required by the tasks and available on the pilot. When the pilot has fewer available cores than what is required by the workload, a group of tasks are executed sequentially. We call this group of tasks a 'generation'. The number of generations of a workload execution affects the theoretical minimum TTX of that execution. For example, given a workload with 128 single-core, 10 minutes-long tasks and a pilot with 64 cores, the execution of that workload will require 2 generations. The theoretical minimum TTX of 2 $generations \times 10\,min = 20\,min$, assuming 100% RU of the pilot's cores and no RP Agent overhead.

It is fundamental to understand that the executable of a unit is irrelevant to the set of experiments performed here: whether a unit runs `sleep`, `stress`, an emulator (e.g., `Synapse`), a simulation kernel (e.g. `Gromacs`) or any other executable has no effect on the measure of the throughput and concurrency of the RP Agent components, or on TTX and RU. This follows from the design and separation of scheduling, launching and execution of a process. The RP Agent schedules and launches a unit and, once launched, the unit executes its code. While the unit is executing, the Executer component of RP Agent will not interact with the unit. What code the unit is executing is completely irrelevant to the Executer and therefore to RP as a whole.

## 5.1   Microbenchmark Experiments

Microbenchmarks measure the performance of individual RP components *in isolation*. In a microbenchmark experiment, RP launches a pilot on a resource with a single unit scheduled onto the Agent. When the unit enters the component under investigation, it is cloned a specified number of times—10000 for experiments in this paper. The components operate on the clones, experiencing real loading while being stressed in isolation and independent of other components.

Microbenchmark experiments are designed to isolate a component by eliminating communication, coordination and concurrency with other components. In this way, the benchmarked component does not compete for shared system resources and communication channels, and remains immune from bottlenecks in other components. Thus, the microbenchmark measures the performance *upper bound* of a component implementation, as achieved *in isolation* from all types of overhead as a consequence of interaction with other components.

We perform microbenchmark experiments for the Scheduler and Executer components of RP Agent, the two components that most affect the overall performance of the RP Agent (see Fig. 4). For the Executer, we test two launch methods: ORTE-CLI, and ORTE-LIB. Note that these methods are not used by the **executable** of the units, but instead by the RP component to launch the executable. In turn, the executable could be single/multi-thread/process or use MPI itself. Depending on the launch methods, we run microbenchmarks load-balancing among 2, 4 and 8 Executer instances, executed on 1, 2, 4, and 8 compute nodes.

We perform microbenchmark experiments on *Blue Waters* as the representative Cray system. As noted before, the executable of the units has no bearing on the microbenchmarks. Microbenchmarking of the Scheduler component require no execution, while Executer benchmarking requires actual execution of the units. We use the `sleep` command to avoid any irrelevant complication deriving from setting up specific execution environments.

A full set of microbenchmarks would span a large parameter space, making it unfeasible to present the full set of experimental results. We focus on results which expose performance and scaling differences among the RP Agent components. This enables a better characterization of the overall performance of the Agent.

**Agent Scheduler Performance.** Currently, RP can instantiate exactly one Scheduler component per Agent. The Scheduler is compute and communication bound: the scheduling algorithm searches repeatedly through the list of managed cores, while core assignment and deassignment are handled in separate, message-driven threads.

Figure 6(a) shows the performance of the Scheduler component in assigning cores to one generation of single-core units, for four pilot sizes. We see that the throughput is dependent on the pilot size, and that the throughput rate declines as more units are scheduled. This is explained by the chosen scheduling algorithm and its implementation: the fewer free cores remain, the more work needs to be done by the scheduling algorithm to find a suitable set of cores for the next units. This behavior is a consequence of using one scheduler to handle workloads with both homogeneous and heterogeneous units (single/multi-core, mpi, cpu/gpu, etc.). In Sect. 5.3, we show how a special-purpose scheduler drastically improves performance.

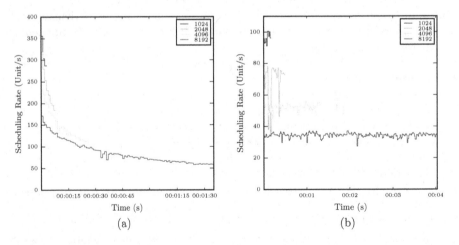

**Fig. 6.** RP Agent Scheduler component throughput as function of time. 1 generation of single-core units on 4 pilot sizes. **(a)** allocating cores to a unit; **(b)** both allocating cores to a unit and deallocating those cores from the units (steady state).

Figure 6(b) shows the same workload of the previous microbenchmark experiment, but the measurements also include the operations of unscheduling units and freeing cores (i.e., steady state scheduler). We do not observe the slope of Fig. 6(a) because both the scheduling and unscheduling operations contend the lock on the Scheduler data structure. This considerably reduces the performance of the Scheduler when compared to only allocating cores to the units.

**Unit Execution Performance.** RP can instantiate multiple Executer component instances per Agent. The Executor's performance is bound by the launch methods used to spawn the units for execution. Currently, RP supports four launch methods on Cray (ALPS, CCM, ORTE-CLI, and ORTE-LIB). Only the two ORTE-based methods enable single/multi-core units within and across compute nodes to run, at scales comparable to the size of *Blue Waters* and *Titan*.

Figure 7 (top) shows the scaling behavior of the ORTE-CLI launch method. Throughput scales with the number of Executer components, with each component running on a dedicated compute node. Data for experiments with increasing instances per node are not presented, as no performance improvements were observed. This suggests that the current performance of the Executer component using ORTE-CLI has an upper-bound due to interaction with the OS.

While ORTE-CLI did not scale with multiple instances of an Executer component on a single compute-node, Fig. 7 (bottom) shows that with the ORTE-LIB launch method, performance scales with up to 4 instances per node. Adding more instances does not increase the performance further. This suggests that 4 Executer components on 1 compute node and the ORTE-LIB launch method reach the performance upper-bound of the ORTE layer.

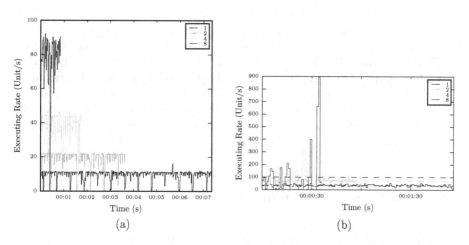

**Fig. 7.** Throughput of 1–8 RP Agent Executer components with 2 launch mechanisms. **(a)** ORTE-CLI, 1–8 Executer components, each run on 1 compute node. **(b)** ORTE-LIB, 1–8 instances, all run on the same MOM node.

Figure 8 shows the scaling of the ORTE-LIB launch method for different pilot sizes. We launch 1024, 2048, 4096 and 8192 single-core units on pilots with 1024, 2048, 4096 and 8192 cores. Throughput is stable over time but jittery with a mean (std. dev) of 48.2 (10.2), 42.6 (7.1), 39.1 (9.8) unit/s. The jitter is explained by the interaction with many external system components which, in their totality, introduce significant noise.

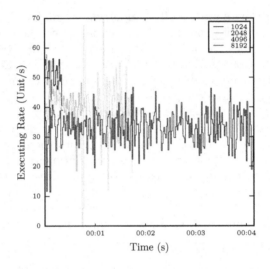

**Fig. 8.** Throughput of 1 RP Agent Executer component with ORTE-LIB launch method; 1024, 2048, 4096 and 8192 cores/units.

The best performance of ORTE-CLI is lower than the performance of the Scheduler for a pilot with up to 1024 cores, as seen in Fig. 6. This indicates that ORTE-CLI creates a bottleneck at the launching stage in the Agent's Executer. In absolute terms, the performance of ORTE-LIB is lower than the scheduling component's when the pilot size is less than 8192 cores, and comparable (or at times higher) at pilot sizes over 8192 cores. Similar to the Scheduler component, the performance decreases with increased pilot size, from an average rate of around 48 units/s for the 1024 pilot size to an average rate of around 33 units/s for larger pilots.

## 5.2   Agent Integrated Performance

To characterize the RP Agent performance as a whole, we employ workloads with varying unit durations executed on pilots of different sizes. The size of each unit is set to 1 core, allowing experiments to measure the performance of RP with maximum pilot cores/unit ratio. Workloads with multi-core units lower the overall stress on the components of the Agents and their communication and coordination protocols, resulting in better performance.

Microbenchmarks are not sufficient to characterize the Agent performance as a whole for three reasons: (i) by definition, the microbenchmarks in section "Unit Execution Performance" and section "Agent Scheduler Performance" cannot measure the performance cost of communication among components; (ii) the concurrent operation of multiple components introduces competition for shared system resources (e.g., competing for filesystem access); and (iii) the Agent performance can be limited by components or system resources *outside* of the Agent (e.g., RP client manager components, or network latency between the Agent and MongoDB).

Accordingly, the set of integration experiments discussed in this subsection investigates the contributions of communication and concurrency to the Agent performance. To offset external overheads, we design the experiments so that the Agent operates independent of the performance of the PilotManager and UnitManager components (Fig. 4): we introduce a startup barrier in the Agent to ensure that the Agent receives sufficient work to fully utilize the pilot's resources. In this way, the Agent starts to process units only when the complete workload has arrived at the Agent.

On *Blue Waters*, we measure time-dependent concurrency achieved by the RP Agent for pilots with 2048, 4096, 8192, and 16384 cores. For each pilot size, the workload is comprised of 3 generations of single-core units, resulting in workloads with 6144, 12288, 24576, and 49152 units. For each workload, the duration of each unit is 64, 128 and 256 s, long enough for all the units of the first generation to start before the first unit is completed. In this way, the first generation can always reach maximum concurrency, saturating the number of cores available on the pilot.

Figure 9 shows the maximal concurrency for each pilot size, where all cores are simultaneous used to execute units. The initial slope up to that maximum concurrency is determined by the performance of the scheduler, which, as shown in Fig. 6(a), is dependent on the pilot size. For example, with the 8192-core pilot we see that 8192 units are started in about 100 s. This is comparable to what is shown in figure Fig. 6(a), where 8192 units are scheduled in about 90 s, with a throughput which starts out at 150 units/s and later stabilizes at about 50 units/s.

Figure 9 shows also that once the first generation of units begins to finish execution, the scheduler enters a different mode of operation where scheduling and unscheduling threads compete (see discussion of Fig. 6(b)). This decreases the overall throughput of the Agent which is no longer able to maintain full concurrency. This effect is independent of pilot size and number of units.

**Comparing ORTE to ALPS and CCM.** One of the limitations of ALPS/APRUN is that we can only run one unit per node. SSH based launch methods in CCM-mode on *Blue Waters* are also limited, due to connection limits when executing more than 8 concurrent units per node. ORTE does not have that limitation. In order to keep the runs comparable, i.e., to execute the same configurations for all experiments, we configure the workload used to use 32 cores per unit, so that each unit consumes a full node. This workload can be executed with all RP launch methods.

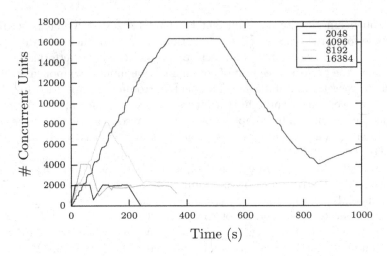

**Fig. 9.** Unit concurrency as a function of pilot size and unit duration.

On *Blue Waters*, we run 10 workloads ranging from 3 to 768 units, where each unit consumes a full compute node (32 cores) and executes on pilots ranging form 32 cores (1 node) to 8192 cores (256 nodes) respectively. We run the same set of 10 workloads for each launch method and compare the actual Time to Execution (TTX) against the theoretically optimal TTX (i.e., the time taken by all the units to execute without any RP overhead).

Figure 10 shows that there is a large trend difference between ORTE-CLI/ORTE-LIB and ALPS/CCM. As the scale increases, the difference between

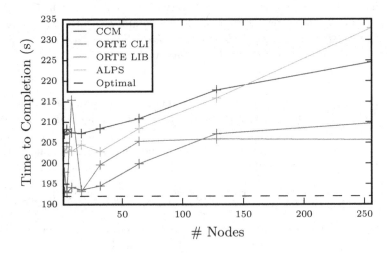

**Fig. 10.** Time to Execution (TTX) as a function of number of units, size of pilot and Executer launch method.

ALPS/CCM to ORTE increases, with ORTE being closer to the theoretically optimal TTX and ALPS/CCM increasing somewhat linearly after around 50 nodes.

## 5.3   Resource Utilization and Overheads at Scale

Currently, the ORTE launch method is the one supporting the largest runs with RP on Cray machines, allowing to execute workloads with 16384 multi-core units on more than 130000 cores. We run two experiments to characterize the weak and strong scaling behavior of RP and its overheads up to this scale. In the weak scaling experiment, we execute workloads with a constant ratio between units and cores. In the strong scaling experiment, we execute one workload on a progressively larger amount of cores. In this way, the strong scaling experiment executes the workload with between 2 and 32 generations.

Weak and strong scaling experiments execute workloads with 32 cores, 15 min long MPI tasks. We perform both experiments on *Titan* for two main reasons: (i) *Titan* is very similar to *Blue Waters* in terms of architecture and scale; and (ii) these experiments required around 25 million core-hours, at the time available only on *Titan*.

Figure 11 shows both the weak (first 8 bars) and strong (last 3 bars) scaling experiments. We measure resource utilization as percentage of the available core-time spent executing the workload (Workload Execution, central portion of the stacked bar), RP code (RP Overhead, lower portion of the stacked bar), or idling (RP Idle, top portion of the stacked bar). Runs measuring weak scaling with between 32/1024 and 128/4096 tasks/cores have a relatively constant percentage of core-time utilization but this percentage decreases with the growing of the number of tasks/cores. As a result, we observe that RP Agent does not weak scale with pilot larger than 8192 cores.

Runs measuring strong scaling show values of RP overhead and idling inversely proportional to the number of generations: the more generations, the less overhead and idling. This is explained by noting that, when tasks of one generation terminate, those of the following generation immediately starts

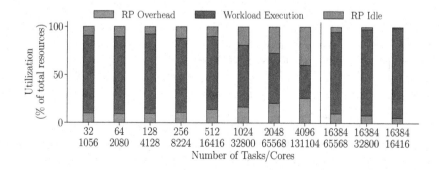

**Fig. 11.** Resource utilization of RADICAL-Pilot.

executing. This eliminates the idling of cores for all generations but the last one. We presume that the increase of RP overhead depends, at least to some extent, on the proportional relation between the communication required to coordinate an execution and the size of the pilot used.

**Reducing RP Overhead.** We explore the decrease in resource utilization measured in the weak scaling experiment (Fig. 11, first 8 bars) by looking at the results of the microbenchmark shown in Fig. 6, and focusing on the relation between scheduling performance and size of the pilot used for the execution.

As described in Sect. 5.1, the larger the pilot, the larger is the resource pool managed by the scheduler. Currently, the scheduler is implemented to repeatedly search a Python data structure for available cores. This approach is effective for a general purpose scheduler that needs to handle many types of workload—e.g., homogeneous/heterogeneous, MPI/OpenMP/Scalar, or single-node/multi-node. However, for homogeneous workloads, a more efficient single-purpose scheduler can be implemented.

Leveraging the flexibility and extensibility of RP (as also used for the Executer and its multiple launch methods), we implemented a scheduler algorithm which specifically handles homogeneous, multi-node tasks of workloads used in weak and strong scaling experiments. The behavior of this special purpose scheduler is shown in Fig. 12 the scheduler manages each task in constant time, at a much lower time per task compared to the general-purpose scheduler.

When the special purpose scheduler encounters the first unit to schedule, it immediately divides the total set of cores into partitions which are all of the same size as the number of cores required by the first unit. In this way, the scheduling algorithm is reduced to the procedure of assigning equally-sized partitions to the units as they arrive. Crucially, this avoid the need for any search on a (Python) data structure representing the cores managed by the pilot. Instead, partition lookup and assignment can be performed in constant time.

It should be noted that there still remain limitations for when the second generations of units gets scheduled, i.e., when the scheduling and unscheduling processes compete. Nonetheless, the throughput of this scheduler is consistently higher than for the general-purpose scheduler: the lock contention reduces due

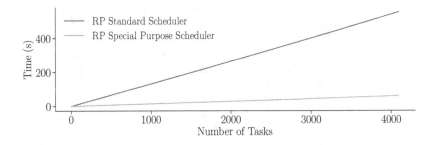

**Fig. 12.** Scheduling overheads: Standard and special purpose schedulers.

to the reduced time for which the scheduler algorithm needs to lock the data structures. Full details on the homogeneous bag of task scheduler and more detailed measurements are discussed in [23].

## 5.4 Discussion

Microbenchmark experiments provide insight on how the Agent's Scheduler and Executer components perform for different Agent configurations and pilot sizes (Sect. 5.1). These experiments provide an upper-bound of the throughput (i.e., units handled per second) of each of the two components and show which component could be the rate-determining factor in the overall agent integrated performance scales. Microbenchmark experiments for the Agent's Scheduler component show that the scheduling throughput is dependent on the pilot size, and that the throughput rate declines as more units are scheduled. Further, we show that when the component is doing both the scheduling and unscheduling operations (i.e., scheduler reaches steady state) the scheduler's throughput is primarily dependent on the pilot size as seen in Fig. 6(b), viz., as the pilot size increases, the scheduler's throughput decreases.

The microbenchmark experiments with the Executer component show that its throughput decreases when the pilot size and unit counts increase in the same proportion, similar to what was observed for the Scheduler component. For both ORTE-CLI and ORTE-LIB Executer launch methods we show increased throughput when an increasing number of concurrent executers are used. ORTE-LIB allows multiple executers on the MOM node, while ORTE-CLI requires a compute node for each executer. As described in Sect. 4.3, this is explained by observing that an execution through ORTE-LIB is only a library call that causes a network call and doesn't strain the system on which it is running. Conversely, each execution call done through ORTE-CLI requires interactions with the filesystem and network resources to communicate with the orte-dvm. Thus an agent using ORTE-CLI reaches the resource limits of *Blue Waters* and Titan with workloads that consists of very large numbers of concurrent tasks or when running multiple components on the same MOM node.

Section 5.2 describes experiments that characterize the integrated performance of RP Agent. We show that the maximal concurrency achievable for multiple pilot sizes, where all cores are simultaneously used to execute units, is approximately 16000 units. We also compare the performance of the ALPS, CCM and ORTE Executer launch methods and found that ORTE-LIB and ORTE-CLI launch methods out-perform ALPS and CCM for the performance metric of TTX. We also show that the performance of ORTE-CLI and ORTE-LIB launch methods are comparable when the number of units is between 3 and 768 units, but this is likely to change with a higher number of units, where configurations with multiple executers and the lower impact of ORTE-LIB on resource utilization would make the ORTE-LIB launch method perform better than ORTE-CLI. Further, we note that the performance of CCM on *Blue Waters* is low compared to other launch methods available on non-Cray HPC systems like Stampede [24].

Finally, we measured the resource utilization of RP Agent at highest scale currently supported, both in terms of number of units concurrently executed and number of cores of a single pilot. We moved from a single-core units to units of 32-cores, and we ran weak scaling experiments with workloads ranging from 32 to 4096 units on pilot sizes ranging from 32 to 131104 cores respectively, and strong scaling experiments with workloads of 16384 units on pilot sizes ranging from 16416 to 65568 cores (Sect. 5.3). Our experiments show that resource utilization of the RP Agent for the weak scaling experiments with pilot sizes between of 1024 and 4096 cores have a relatively constant percentage of core-time utilization, but this percentage significantly decreases with pilots larger than 8192 cores. We attributed RP Agent's poor weak scaling property with pilot sizes over 8192 cores to the performance of the Agent Scheduler component.

We addressed the decrease in resource utilization measured in the weak scaling experiment and showed the flexibility and extensibility or RP, by implementing a special-purpose scheduler, specific to the experimental workload— i.e., homogeneous, multi-node tasks. We then showed that the overhead added by the special-purpose scheduler significantly decreases compared to the one of the special-purpose scheduler used for the experiment.

# 6   Conclusion

*Prima facie*, a system implementing the Pilot abstraction [2,25] provides the conceptual and functional capabilities needed to support the scalable execution of many task workloads. The impact of an abstraction is limited to its best implementation. Whereas there are several existent pilot systems, they are either geared towards specific functionality or platforms. This paper describes the architecture and implementation of RP (Sect. 3.1), and characterizes the performance of its Agent module on Cray platforms (Sect. 5).

In molecular sciences, there is a demonstrated need [26] to be able to support up to $10^5$ MPI tasks as part of a single "ensemble simulation". Similar scales are anticipated across multiple domains. Several parts of RP will need to be re-engineered to efficiently execute workloads at this scale. Most of the benefits will come from improving the Agent, as discussed in Sect. 3.1 and consistent with results shown in Sect. 5. To this end, we are planning to: (i) develop a set of specialized, lock-free schedulers; (ii) partition the pilot resources and operate multiple agents in parallel on these partitions; (iii) explore new launch methods; and (iv) aggregate units depending on their application provenance and duration to optimize Scheduler and Executor throughput.

The focus of this paper has been on the direct execution of workloads on HPC machines, but RP also serves as the runtime system for a range of other tools and libraries [27–30], many already used in production. The requirements of these tools and libraries will also motivate future research and development.

## Software and Data
RP is available for immediate use on many platforms [31]. RP source is accompanied with extensive documentation and an active developer-user community.

Source code, raw data and analysis scripts to reproduce experiments can be found at:

- RADICAL-Pilot: https://github.com/radical-cybertools/radical.pilot
- RADICAL-Analytics: https://github.com/radical-cybertools/radical.analytics
- Data and scripts: https://github.com/radical-experiments/jsspp18

**Acknowledgments.** This work is supported by NSF "CAREER" ACI-1253644, NSF ACI-1440677 "RADICAL-Cybertools" and DOE Award DE-SC0016280. We acknowledge access to computational facilities: XSEDE resources (TG-MCB090174) and Blue Waters (NSF-1713749).

# References

1. Hwang, E., Kim, S., Yoo, T.K., Kim, J.S., Hwang, S., Choi, Y.R.: Resource allocation policies for loosely coupled applications in heterogeneous computing systems. IEEE Trans. Parallel Distrib. Syst. **27**(8), 2349–2362 (2016)
2. Turilli, M., Santcroos, M., Jha, S.: A comprehensive perspective on Pilot-Jobs. ACM Comput. Surv. (2017, accepted, in press). http://arxiv.org/abs/1508.04180
3. Preto, J., Clementi, C.: Fast recovery of free energy landscapes via diffusion-map-directed molecular dynamics. Phys. Chem. Chem. Phys. **16**(36), 19181–19191 (2014)
4. Cheatham III, T.E., Roe, D.R.: The impact of heterogeneous computing on workflows for biomolecular simulation and analysis. Comput. Sci. Eng. **17**(2), 30–39 (2015)
5. Sugita, Y., Okamoto, Y.: Replica-exchange molecular dynamics method for protein folding. Chem. Phys. Lett. **314**(1), 141–151 (1999)
6. Pordes, R., et al.: The open science grid. J. Phys. Conf. Ser. **78**(1), 012057 (2007)
7. Maeno, T., et al.: Evolution of the ATLAS PanDA workload management system for exascale computational science. J. Phys. Conf. Ser. **513**(3), 032062 (2014). Proceedings of the 20th International Conference on Computing in High Energy and Nuclear Physics (CHEP 2013)
8. Raicu, I., Zhao, Y., Dumitrescu, C., Foster, I., Wilde, M.: Falkon: a Fast and Light-weight tasK executiON framework. In: Proceedings of the 8th ACM/IEEE Conference on Supercomputing, p. 43. ACM (2007)
9. Wilde, M., Hategan, M., Wozniak, J.M., Clifford, B., Katz, D.S., Foster, I.: Swift: a language for distributed parallel scripting. Parallel Comput. **37**(9), 633–652 (2011)
10. CCM. http://bit.ly/cray_ccm. Accessed Jan 2018
11. Karo, M., Lagerstrom, R., Kohnke, M., Albing, C.: The application level placement scheduler (2006)
12. Castain, R.H., Squyres, J.M.: Creating a transparent, distributed, and resilient computing environment: the OpenRTE project. J. Supercomput. **42**(1), 107–123 (2007)
13. TaskFarmer. http://bit.ly/taskfarmer
14. Wraprun. https://www.olcf.ornl.gov/kb_articles/wraprun/
15. QDO. http://bit.ly/nersc_qdo
16. Canon, R.S., Ramakrishnan, L., Srinivasan, J.: My Cray can do that? Supporting diverse workloads on the Cray XE-6. In: Cray User Group (2012)

17. Python Task Farm. http://www.archer.ac.uk/documentation/user-guide/batch.php#sec-5.7
18. Ahn, D.H., Garlick, J., Grondona, M., Lipari, D., Springmeyer, B., Schulz, M.: Flux: a next-generation resource management framework for large HPC centers. In: 2014 43rd International Conference on Parallel Processing Workshops (ICCPW), pp. 9–17. IEEE (2014)
19. Merzky, A., Weidner, O., Jha, S.: SAGA: a standardized access layer to heterogeneous distributed computing infrastructure. Software-X (2015). https://doi.org/10.1016/j.softx.2015.03.001
20. Santcroos, M., Castain, R., Merzky, A., Bethune, I., Jha, S.: Executing dynamic heterogeneous workloads on blue waters with radical-pilot. In: Cray User Group 2016 (2016)
21. PMIx web site. https://www.open-mpi.org/projects/pmix/
22. CFFI Documentation. http://cffi.readthedocs.org
23. Merzky, A., Turilli, M., Maldonado, M., Jha, S.: Design and performance characterization of RADICAL-pilot on titan. arXiv preprint arXiv:1801.01843 (2018)
24. Merzky, A., Santcroos, M., Turilli, M., Jha, S.: Executing dynamic and heterogeneous workloads on super computers (2016, under review). http://arxiv.org/abs/1512.08194
25. Luckow, A., Santcroos, M., Merzky, A., Weidner, O., Mantha, P., Jha, S.: P*: a model of pilot-abstractions. In: IEEE 8th International Conference on e-Science, pp. 1–10 (2012). https://doi.org/10.1109/eScience.2012.6404423
26. Jha, S., Kasson, P.M.: High-level software frameworks to surmount the challenge of 100x scaling for biomolecul ar simulation science. White Paper submitted to NIH-NSF Request for Information (2015). https://doi.org/10.5281/zenodo.44377
27. Balasubramanian, V., Treikalis, A., Weidner, O., Jha, S.: Ensemble toolkit: scalable and flexible execution of ensembles of tasks. In: 2016 45th International Conference on Parallel Processing (ICPP), vol. 00, pp. 458–463, August 2016
28. Treikalis, A., Merzky, A., Chen, H., Lee, T.S., York, D.M., Jha, S.: RepEx: a flexible framework for scalable replica exchange molecular dynamics simulations. In: 2016 45th International Conference on Parallel Processing (ICPP), August 2016
29. Balasubramanian, V., et al.: Harnessing the power of many: extensible toolkit for scalable ensemble applications (2017). https://arxiv.org/abs/1710.08491
30. Balasubramanian, V., et al.: ExTASY: scalable and flexible coupling of MD simulations and advanced sampling techniques. In: 2016 IEEE 12th International Conference on e-Science (e-Science), pp. 361–370, October 2016
31. RADICAL-Pilot. https://github.com/radical-cybertools/radical.pilot

# Adaptive Simultaneous Multi-tenancy for GPUs

Ramin Bashizade[(✉)], Yuxuan Li, and Alvin R. Lebeck

Department of Computer Science, Duke University, Durham, NC, USA
{ramin,alvy}@cs.duke.edu, yuxuanlala@gmail.com

**Abstract.** Graphics Processing Units (GPUs) are energy-efficient massively parallel accelerators that are increasingly deployed in multi-tenant environments such as data-centers for general-purpose computing as well as graphics applications. Using GPUs in multi-tenant setups requires an efficient and low-overhead method for sharing the device among multiple users that improves system throughput while adapting to the changes in workload. This requires mechanisms to control the resources allocated to each kernel, and an efficient policy to make decisions about this allocation.

In this paper, we propose adaptive simultaneous multi-tenancy to address these issues. Adaptive simultaneous multi-tenancy allows for sharing the GPU among multiple kernels, as opposed to single kernel multi-tenancy that only runs one kernel on the GPU at any given time and static simultaneous multi-tenancy that does not adapt to events in the system. Our proposed system dynamically adjusts the kernels' parameters at run-time when a new kernel arrives or a running kernel ends. Evaluations using our prototype implementation show that, compared to sequentially executing the kernels, system throughput is improved by an average of 9.8% (and up to 22.4%) for combinations of kernels that include at least one low-utilization kernel.

## 1 Introduction

Graphics Processing Units (GPUs) are massively parallel accelerators that were originally intended to execute graphics applications, but their high throughput and energy-efficiency motivates their use by broader application domains. Numerous cloud service providers offer GPUs as part of their solutions [2,9,15]. In such environments a large number of kernels with different memory access and compute behaviors request running on GPUs. Running only one kernel on the GPU in these environments underutilizes resources, since a single kernel cannot utilize all the resources on the device most of the time [21]. Therefore, always dedicating the entire GPU to only one customer (or single kernel) is not cost-efficient either for the service provider or for the customer. One example to address this issue is Amazon Web Services' plan to provide fractional GPUs (Elastic GPUs [2]) for applications that have high compute, storage or memory needs that still could benefit from additional GPU resources. Another example

© Springer Nature Switzerland AG 2019
D. Klusáček et al. (Eds.): JSSPP 2018, LNCS 11332, pp. 83–106, 2019.
https://doi.org/10.1007/978-3-030-10632-4_5

is the NVIDIA Volta architecture's support for statically dividing the GPU into multiple smaller virtual GPUs [20].

Sequential execution of kernels on GPUs in multi-tenant environments, such as data-centers, leads to long wait times and reduces system throughput. Overcoming this limitation requires a method for sharing the device among multiple users that is efficient and adaptive to the events in the system (i.e., arrival and departure of kernels.) NVIDIA GPUs support simultaneous execution of multiple kernels and memory operations in a single application via Hyper-Q technology [17]. In addition, the CUDA Multi-Process Service (MPS) [18] facilitates concurrent execution of kernels and memory operations from different applications. However, the first-come-first-served (FCFS) and left-over resource allocation policies make concurrent execution on existing GPUs inefficient. The reason is that the FCFS policy creates a head-of-line blocking situation where the running kernel blocks other kernels until it has all its thread blocks mapped to Streaming Multi-processors (SMs). Additionally, simply allocating the left-over resources of the running kernel to the waiting kernels might not be the optimal solution, since such a policy ignores the different requirements of the kernels and only depends on the order in which the kernels arrive at the GPU. The Volta architecture tries to overcome this head-of-line blocking by adding the capability to statically divide the GPU into smaller virtual GPUs, but the above problems apply to each virtual GPU.

An effective and low-overhead scheme for sharing the GPU among multiple kernels should address both the resource underutilization and the adaptiveness issues. This requires overcoming the head-of-line blocking problem in thread block scheduling on the GPU to address the adaptiveness problem, and having a simple yet effective policy for resource allocation to tackle the underutilization issue. Previous work attempted to support multi-tenancy on the GPU either by a software-based approach [6,30] or by adding the necessary hardware support [22,27]. These works solely support preemption to make the system responsive, i.e., to force low-priority kernels to yield control of the GPU to high-priority kernels, and hence, do not alleviate the resource underutilization problem. A different class of work addresses multi-tasking on the GPU by modifying the hardware [1,12,14,23,28,31] or artificially fusing the kernels from different applications together [10,14,21,29]. In the hardware-based work, the resource allocation policy is fixed and cannot be changed. Furthermore, most of the necessary hardware support is not present in existing GPUs. Software-based approaches that rely on merging applications together are impractical in real world scenarios since it requires merging every possible combination of kernels beforehand. Our work does not suffer from these shortcomings since we use a low-overhead software approach to solve the GPU multi-tenancy problem at run-time.

These challenges inspired us to design a system that realizes multi-tenancy for commodity GPUs. In this paper, we propose adaptive simultaneous multi-tenancy for GPUs. Our system dynamically adjusts the resources allocated to kernels based on the requirements of all kernels requesting execution on the GPU at run-time. We achieve this by adopting a cooperative approach between applications and a host-side service, supported via minimal application modifications and a lightweight API. Our approach focuses on a single server, as the problem of assigning work to specific servers in data-centers is addressed elsewhere [24]. Therefore, we assume that the work assigned to this machine is optimized by the higher level scheduler.

In our proposed system, we manage the resources allocated to each kernel, and control the mapping of kernels' thread blocks to SMs. Naively applying resource allocation policies can lead to unintended mappings of thread blocks to SMs and result in further underutilization of resources. To avoid this, we build on the concept of persistent threads [11] with a few modifications to implement our desired mapping policy on the GPU. Our work differs from previous work that uses persistent threads to support preemption [6,30] in that we show how to control the assignment of thread blocks to SMs and use it to have control over resource allocation to kernels. Moreover, support for preemption comes almost for free when we adopt this approach.

To realize adaptive simultaneous multi-tenancy, we implement a host-side service with which applications communicate to obtain launch parameters for their kernels. The service monitors the kernels running on the GPU and makes decisions for launch parameters based on the adopted allocation policy. In this work, we use offline profiling of kernels and implement a greedy policy using this data with the goal of minimizing the maximum execution time among all running kernels, or in other words, maximizing system throughput (STP). We show that using our design, STP is improved by an average of 9.8% (and up to 22.4%) for combinations of kernels that include at least one low-utilization kernel, with respect to the sequential execution of the kernels. Compared to a system in which persistent threads transformation is applied to the kernels, the average STP improvement for these kernel combinations is 4.3%. We do not compare our system with other software-based multi-tenant systems [6,30], since the target of those systems is to improve the turnaround time of high-priority kernels whereas our goal in this work is to improve the throughput of the whole system. Improving STP, assuming Service Level Agreements (SLAs) are not violated, translates into less energy consumption of the data-center by allowing for reduction in the number of servers for the same amount of work, or in higher scalability by doing more work with the same number of servers, both of which are crucial factors in determining the Total Cost of Ownership (TCO) [4].

We make the following contributions in this paper:

- We identify the need for sharing the GPU among multiple kernels by characterizing the behavior of a set of benchmark kernels. Our observations show that running only one kernel at a time leads to underutilization of different types of resources on the GPU. On the other hand, simply running two kernels together without considering resource utilization does not realize the potential STP gains.

- We use the concept of persistent threads to control the resources allocated to each kernel at run-time. This allows us to solve the head-of-line blocking at the GPU block scheduler[1].
- We design and implement an adaptive simultaneous multi-tenant prototype system that runs on current GPUs. Adaptive simultaneous multi-tenancy is a generalization of single-kernel multi-tenancy [6,30], and static simultaneous multi-tenancy supported by the NVIDIA Volta architecture, in which the GPU is shared by multiple kernels at the same time based on the requirements of all kernels. Our system is composed of a host-side service that makes decisions regarding the allocation of resources to kernels and preemption/relaunch of running kernels, and an application-side API that encapsulates the communications with the service in a few function calls.
- We evaluate the proposed system for a set of benchmark kernels using a full prototype on real GPUs and show the effectiveness of our approach in terms of improving STP.

The rest of this paper is organized as follows. A brief background about GPU execution model as well as motivation for our work are presented in Sect. 2. Section 3 elaborates our proposed system. Evaluation methodology and experimental results are discussed in Sect. 4. Section 5 covers the related work. Finally, Sect. 6 concludes the paper.

## 2   Background and Motivation

### 2.1   GPU Execution Model

GPUs are massively parallel accelerators that are composed of thousands of simple cores. A large number of cores together with cache, shared memory[2], register files, and some other components form streaming multi-processors (SMs). All SMs share a last level cache. Figure 1a and b show the architecture of and SM and the GPU.

Figure 1c illustrates the structure of a kernel. GPU kernels comprise a large number of threads that execute the same instructions on different data, hence the name Single-Instruction-Multiple-Thread (SIMT). These threads are grouped together to form thread blocks, and a set of thread blocks is called a grid. All thread blocks in a grid have the same dimensions, and all threads of the same thread block can only run on a single SM. A thread block is a logical notion that helps the programmers reason about their code. However, a limited number of thread blocks can fit on the device at the same time. We separate these concepts and refer to the physical thread blocks actually running on the GPU as concurrent thread arrays (CTAs). Note that in some other works thread blocks and CTAs are used interchangeably.

---

[1] The recently announced NVIDIA Volta architecture solves the head-of-line blocking at the GPU block scheduler by dividing the GPU into smaller virtual GPUs, but it lacks the flexibility provided by persistent threads.

[2] Scratchpad memory in NVIDIA terminology is called shared memory.

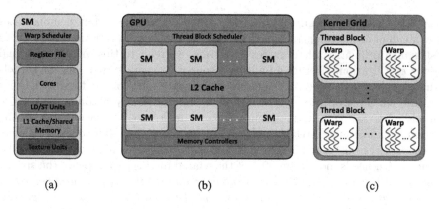

**Fig. 1.** (a) SM components, (b) GPU components, and (c) kernel structure.

When there are enough resources on an SM to host a waiting thread block, the block scheduler dispatches that thread block to the available SM for execution. If there are more than one SM with enough resources, the mapping happens in a round-robin fashion. In each SM then, warp scheduler dispatches ready warps to execute instructions. A warp is the smallest group of threads that execute in lockstep to reduce the overhead of instruction fetch and control flow. The programmer has no control over the size of a warp. Once a thread block is mapped to an SM, it continues execution until it finishes. In other words, there is no mechanism for preemption or yielding resources (the Pascal [19] and Volta [20] architectures perform context switching, but the programmer does not have control over the operation).

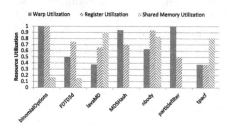

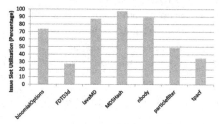

**Fig. 2.** Spatial utilization of different resources in SMs for the benchmark kernels.

**Fig. 3.** Issue slot utilization for the benchmark kernels.

## 2.2   Resource Requirements

Figure 2 shows the amount of SM resources occupied by the benchmark kernels. The data are obtained from the system described in Sect. 4.1 using NVIDIA profiler and the details of the benchmarks are discussed in Sect. 4.2. This figure does not show how often each of these resources are used, but demonstrates how much of each type is occupied by kernels when run in isolation. In order to distinguish utilization of resources over time, we refer to this metric as spatial resource utilization. There is a limiting resource for every kernel, i.e., the kernels exhaust one or two types of resources while there are more of the other types left unused. This creates opportunities to simultaneously accommodate more kernels with complementary requirements to maximize the throughput of the system. For instance, MD5Hash kernel needs more than 70% of the registers on the device, but uses no shared memory. It can be combined with lavaMD kernel which needs more than 90% of the shared memory to improve the spatial resource utilization of the GPU. *Taking advantage of this opportunity requires a method that shares each SM among multiple kernels, because sharing the GPU among multiple kernels while each SM is dedicated to a single kernel does not alleviate the SM resource underutilization.*

### 2.3    Issue Slot Utilization

A different metric for utilization is Issue Slot Utilization (ISU). ISU refers to the percentage of issue slots that issued at least one instruction. It is an indication of how busy the kernel keeps the device. Figure 3 shows ISU for the benchmark kernels. The contrast between ISU and spatial resource utilization is visible in Figs. 2 and 3. Figure 2 suggested that MD5Hash and lavaMD are good candidates to be combined together for throughput improvement, whereas Fig. 3 shows that both kernels keep the device busy more that 70% of the time. Thus, although the resource requirements of the two kernels are complementary, there are not many stall cycles during the execution of each of them that the other kernel can take advantage of. Based on the ISU values, lavaMD and tpacf are better candidates to run together, because despite their similar resource requirements, they have complementary ISUs. On the other hand, without complementary resource requirement, it is impossible to fit both kernels on the GPU. *Therefore, an efficient solution is needed to tune the resources allocated to each kernel such that the requirements for both metrics are met.*

### 2.4    Non-overlapping Execution

CUDA MPS [18] combines multiple CUDA contexts into one to allow for simultaneous execution of multiple kernels from different applications on the GPU. However, our observations show that the block scheduling algorithm on the GPU does not properly take advantage of this capability. This issue is covered in prior work too [6]. When multiple applications want to launch kernels on the GPU, their thread blocks are queued in the order they have arrived at the device. As the resources become available by completion of older thread blocks, newer ones are assigned to SMs. This FCFS policy leads to a head-of-line blocking situation where more resource-consuming kernels that arrived earlier block the execution of less resource-consuming kernels, even though there might be enough resources to accommodate thread blocks of the smaller kernels. To address this issue, we use persistent threads [11] to restrict the number of CTAs of each kernel on the device, thus constraining the resources it uses.

To summarize, the challenges to sharing a GPU among multiple kernels are (i) managing the resources allocated to each kernel such that the GPU can accommodate all the kernels at the same time, (ii) allocating resources to kernels in order to create complementary utilizations, (iii) addressing the head-of-line blocking at the GPU block scheduler caused by the FCFS policy on the GPU, and (iv) doing all of these at run-time in an adaptive fashion.

## 3    Adaptive Simultaneous Multi-tenancy

Our proposed solution to the challenges mentioned in Sect. 2 is adaptive simultaneous multi-tenancy. This concept is a generalization of single-kernel multi-tenancy proposed in previous work [6,30], and static simultaneous multi-tenancy supported by the NVIDIA Volta architecture [20]. The idea is to adaptively tune the resources allocated to each kernel to accommodate more kernels on the GPU while supporting kernel preemption to enhance the throughput of the multi-tenant system. To this end, we propose kernel code transformations and an application API to add flexibility to kernels, and employ a host-side service that monitors the kernels running on the GPU to make decisions regarding resource allocation which are then communicated to applications. In the rest of this section, we explain the details of our design.

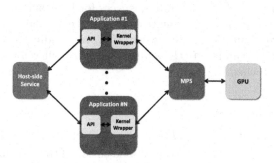

**Fig. 4.** Overview of the proposed adaptive simultaneous multi-tenant system.

### 3.1    Overview

Our proposed system is composed of a host-side service that manages resources allocated to each kernel and determines when kernel adaptation needs to occur, and an API for programmers to utilize the service. Figure 4 shows the overview of the adaptive simultaneous multi-tenant system. On arrival of a new kernel or departure of a running one, the service takes the following actions: (i) it asks the applications for the number of thread blocks their kernels have executed, used in estimation of the remaining execution time. The remaining execution times are used in combination with profiling data in the allocation policy to maximize STP (addressing the challenge in Sect. 2.3); (ii) it computes new parameters for the kernels that are going to run on the GPU. The parameters, which in this work is the number of CTAs but could be extended to different types of resources such as the number registers or the amount of shared memory, must not cause the resources required by the kernels to exceed the available resources on the GPU (addressing challenges in Sects. 2.2 and 2.4); (iii) it communicates the new parameters to the applications.

On the application side, the kernel launch is wrapped inside a function that communicates with the host-side service. We provide an API for the common actions that need to be taken when an application wants to launch a kernel. Ideally these function calls would be included in the CUDA libraries so that the programmer does not have to add anything to their code, but for now they need to be included in the application code manually or via a source-to-source transformation.

In short, the applications that want to run kernels on the GPU have to contact the host-side service using the provided API. The service controls when and which applications should preempt/relaunch kernels and the kernel launch parameters. The kernel launch parameters are passed via the API to the kernel wrapper function that launches the kernel. MPS intercepts kernel calls and merges them in a single context to run on the GPU concurrently. The fact that all concurrent kernels share a virtual address space creates security concerns in a multi-tenant environment. This issue is addressed in the Volta architecture by supporting separation of virtual address spaces for kernels that run on different SMs. Since we share SMs among multiple kernels, this capability does not eliminate the security limitation of our work. However, adding a software address translation layer [25] can isolate the address spaces of different applications with minimal overhead when required.

### 3.2   Host-Side Service

Applications communicate to the service via the API (Sect. 3.3) at two occasions: (i) launching a kernel, and (ii) starting the execution of the last thread block. The reason that we notify the service at this point, and not once the kernel is finished, is that after the last thread block begins execution no changes can be made to the number of CTAs of the kernel. Therefore, by sending the notification before the kernel finishes, we can overlap the communications with and the parameter computation at the host-side service with the execution of the last round of thread blocks of the kernel, effectively hiding the latency of these operations without affecting the number of kernel's CTAs.

The service receives messages on a shared message queue in a loop. Whenever it sees a message in this queue, it keeps reading until the queue is empty to aggregate the effects of back-to-back messages from different applications on the system in a single step. After reading all the messages in the queue, the service opens two dedicated message queues for communications with each client application that has a kernel to run. These queues are used for sending preemption commands and launch parameters, and receiving the progress of the kernel.

When the service is notified by an application of a new event, i.e., a new kernel is arriving or an existing kernel began the execution of its last thread block, it queries other applications for kernel progress via dedicated message queues. Previous work [30] used elapsed time for this purpose, and thus, there was no need to query the application. Nevertheless, this metric is not suitable for our purpose. Elapsed time can be used to measure the progress when only one kernel runs on the GPU at a time, whereas in our proposed system multiple kernels share the device simultaneously and therefore, do not make progress with the same rate as they do when they run in isolation. To overcome this issue, we use the number of executed thread blocks as an indicator of kernel progress.

The service then waits for the response from all applications, as those data are necessary for making allocation decisions. We use asynchronous memory copy operations to overlap these queries with kernel execution. Having the number of executed thread blocks and kernels profiling data, we then estimate the remaining execution time of the kernels (Sect. 3.6). Once this operation is done, the parameters for each kernel are sent to the corresponding application via the dedicated message queues and the application makes the appropriate adjustments.

## 3.3   Application Side

On the application side, we initialize the shared and dedicated message queues, obtain launch parameters for the kernel, wait for notifications from the service for preemption and new launches, and release the resources on completion of the kernel. Table 1 summarizes the application API to support these actions.

**init():** On a kernel launch, the application host code initializes the necessary variables. These include shared and dedicated message queues, necessary memory allocations for communications between the host and the GPU, and streams for asynchronous memory operations and kernel launches. The dedicated message queues are created based on the process ID of the application to ensure uniqueness. There are also pointers to kernel input arguments (kernel_args) that are used when launching a new instance of the kernel.

**obtainParameters():** Once initialization is complete, the host code obtains parameters for the kernel it wants to launch from the host-side service. To this end, it sends a message composed of the kernel name (kernel_name, to retrieve its corresponding profiling data at the host-side service), the names of the dedicated message queues (created using process ID, to open connections to the queues at the service), total number of thread blocks the kernel wants to run (total_blocks, to be used for remaining execution time estimation), dimensions of a thread block (block_dim, to be used for resource usage calculation), and indication that this message is a request for a new kernel (as opposed to notification for the beginning of the execution of the last thread block of an existing kernel). After the message is sent, the host code waits to receive a response from the service.

Once the response arrives, the kernel is launched and two threads are created: one for listening to the host-side service for new launch parameters, and the other for monitoring the progress of the kernel. The first thread uses the stream for memory operations to asynchronously read the number of executed thread blocks from the device and to write to the memory location holding the preemption variable (max_blocks in Fig. 5).

Once a new message with launch parameters comes from the service, there are three possible scenarios: (i) the new number of CTAs is less than what the kernel is currently running with, (ii) new and old numbers of CTAs are equal (i.e., no actions required), or (iii) the new number is greater than the old number of CTAs. In the first case, the thread preempts the proper number of CTAs to match the new parameter by writing to the preemption variable (described in the following section). In the last case, the thread launches a new instance of the kernel on a new stream to run in parallel with the current instance. The second thread is responsible for sending notification to the service once the last thread block of the kernel has started execution.

**release():** Finally, when the kernel finishes, the host code deallocates all the resources used for these communications.

Table 1. Application API.

| Function | Description |
|---|---|
| init(kernel_args) | Initializes the necessary variables for communications with the service and launching new instances of the kernel |
| obtainParameters(kernel_name, total_blocks, block_dim) | Contacts the service with kernel's information and obtains the number of CTAs to launch the kernel. Also upon receiving the response, creates threads for listening to the service and monitoring kernel progress |
| release() | Releases the allocated resources |

### 3.4   Kernel Code Transformation

To have control over the number of CTAs and consequently, the resources allocated to the kernel, we use persistent threads [11]. The concept of persistent threads refers to limiting the number of threads to a value that the GPU can run simultaneously. In addition to control over resources, using persistent threads provides support for preemption at thread-level granularity. Preempting kernels only at thread completion mitigates the need for handling any remaining work due to the preemption.

Using a persistent thread transformation, we override the blockIdx variable in CUDA which refers to the logical thread block index. Figure 5 shows the required transformation to the kernel code to implement persistent threads. It also includes the support for preemption and control over the assignment of CTAs to SMs.

```
1  __global__ void TransformedKernel(/*Original Arguments*/,
2                                    int grid_size,
3                                    int *block_index, int *max_blocks,
4                                    volatile int *concurrent_blocks) {
5      int smid = get_smid();
6      __shared__ int logicalBlockIdx;
7      __shared__ int physicalBlockIdx;
8      if(threadIdx.x == 0) {
9          physicalBlockIdx = atomicAdd(&(block_index[smid + 1]), 1);
10     }
11     __syncthreads();
12     while(physicalBlockIdx < *max_blocks) {
13         if(threadIdx.x == 0) {
14             logicalBlockIdx = atomicAdd(&(block_index[0]), 1);
15             *concurrent_blocks = logicalBlockIdx;
16         }
17         __syncthreads();
18         if(logicalBlockIdx >= grid_size) {
19             break;
20         }
21         /*
22         ...
23         Kernel Code
24         ...
25         */
26     }
27     if(threadIdx.x == 0) {
28         atomicSub(&(block_index[smid + 1]), 1);
29     }
30 }
```

**Fig. 5.** The kernel transformation required for supporting persistent threads and pre-emption.

### 3.5 Profiling and Pruning the Parameter Space

We use offline profiling of kernels in isolation to help estimate the remaining execution time of kernels in a multi-tenant environment, which is used in our allocation policy (Sect. 3.6); we want to minimize the maximum remaining execution time of the kernels to maximize STP. Once the transformation in Sect. 3.4 is applied to the kernel, we can use the number of CTAs as the control knob for the amount of resources allocated to it. After these data have been obtained (we will discuss the results of our profiling in Sect. 4.3), we sort the configuration points based on the number of CTAs and then prune the space such that the execution times of the remaining set of configurations monotonically decrease. Once the pruning is done, we store the remaining set of configurations in an array in the host-side service to be later retrieved by the allocation algorithm. Equation (1) shows how we use the profiling data for estimation of the remaining execution time of the kernel in a multi-tenant environment:

$$T_m^c = T_i^c \times \frac{TB_t - TB_e}{TB_t} \tag{1}$$

In (1), $T_m^c$ is the remaining execution time of the kernel in multi-tenant environment when it is running with $c$ CTAs, $T_i^c$ is its execution time in isolation when it has $c$ CTAs, $TB_t$ is the total number of its thread blocks, and $TB_e$ is the number of thread blocks it has executed so far.

## 3.6  Sharing Policy

Our policy is a greedy method, in which the service starts at the point where all kernels have minimum resources, i.e., one CTA per kernel (line 2 in Algorithm 1.) The algorithm then descendingly sorts the kernels based on their estimated remaining execution times and initializes a variable, marked, to indicate the kernels whose resource allocation is determined (lines 3–4). It then iteratively advances to the next configuration point for the first unmarked kernel (lines 6–7) until all the kernels are marked. If this kernel currently has all the resources it can use, it is marked (line 15) and the loop proceeds to the next iteration. Note that due to sorting the kernels, this operation minimizes the maximum remaining execution time among all kernels. If the new configuration fits the device, i.e., the resources required for it do not exceed those available on the GPU, the kernels are re-sorted and the loop proceeds to the next iteration (lines 8–9). Otherwise, the operation is rolled back and the kernel is marked (lines 11–12). It continues until no kernel can have more resources allocated to it. Note that these steps take place only in the host-side service and the final result is communicated to the applications, i.e., the incremental resource allocation is only in computation, we do not incrementally add to the CTAs a kernel runs with. Algorithm 1 shows the pseudo-code for this policy. If no feasible configuration exists, we simply launch all kernels with one CTA. In this case, kernels will be queued at the block scheduler on the GPU and will start execution once resources become available. The complexity of this algorithm is linear with respect to the

---

**Algorithm 1.** Greedy resource allocation algorithm

---

```
 1: procedure ALLOCATERESOURCES(KernelsList)
 2:     Allocate the minimum resources to each kernel
 3:     Descendingly sort kernels based on their estimated remaining execution times
 4:     marked ← 0
 5:     while marked ≤ KernelsList.size() do
 6:         if KernelsList[marked].nextConfig() then
 7:             KernelsList[marked].advanceToNextConfig()
 8:             if New configurations fit the device then
 9:                 Re-sort the KernelsList from marked onwards
10:             else
11:                 KernelsList[marked].rollBackToPrevConfig()
12:                 marked++
13:             end if
14:         else
15:             marked++
16:         end if
17:     end while
18: end procedure
```

number of configurations of all kernels, i.e., $O(\sum_{k \in K} C_k)$ where $C_k$ is the number of configurations for kernel $k$ and $K$ is the set of all kernels that want to run on the GPU.

It must be noted that any other policy can be easily plugged into our proposed system without affecting any of the parts related to the mechanisms necessary for supporting simultaneous multi-tenancy. The only requirement is that the policy needs to take a list of the kernels and their profiling data as the input and determine configurations for each kernel.

### 3.7  Example Scenario

An example scenario of two applications running kernels on the GPU concurrently is presented in Fig. 6. At step (1), Application #1 contacts the host-side service requesting to run kernel A on the GPU. The service runs the resource allocation algorithm and responds to Application #1 to run kernel A with five CTAs per SM, and consequently Application #1 launches A with the specified number of CTAs.

Then at step (2), Application #2 sends a message to the host-side service and requests to run kernel B on the device. The service queries Application #1 about the progress of kernel A at step (3), and Application #1 responds with the number of thread blocks that A has executed. Based on that information, the service runs the allocation algorithm and sends new launch parameters, i.e., three CTAs for each of A and B, to Applications #1 and #2 at step (4). At this step, Application #1 compares the new number of CTAs with what A is running with currently. Since the new number is smaller than the old one, preemption has to happen. Therefore, Application #1 writes the new value to the max_blocks location mentioned in Sect. 3.4. At the next iteration of the internal loop of A, the last two CTAs at each SM will preempt and make room for CTAs of kernel B. In parallel with this operation, Application #2 launches B with three CTAs per SM. Thread blocks of B will wait at the block scheduler on the GPU until resources become available to start execution.

Once kernel B grabs its last thread block at step (5), Application #2 notifies the host-side service. This triggers running the allocation algorithm again. The service sends new number of CTAs to Application #1, and since the new number is greater than the old one, new CTAs have to be launched. At step (6), Application #1 does so in a separate stream (CTAs inside the dotted rectangle), in order for them to run in parallel with the previous instance of the kernel. Kernel A grabs its last thread block at step (7) and Application #1 notifies the service of this event. Finally, Application #1 is finished and the GPU is empty.

### 3.8  Limitations

A limitation of our work is that the host-side service logically shares a single SM among all kernels, and then extrapolates that configuration to all other

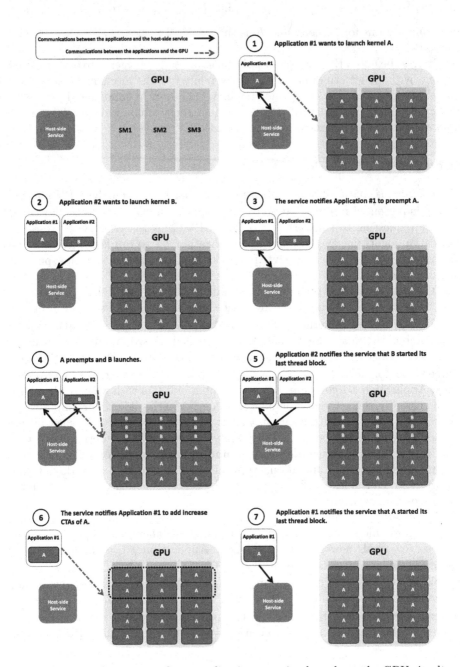

**Fig. 6.** An example scenario of two applications running kernels on the GPU simultaneously.

SMs, although there might be kernels that benefit from having the entire SM to themselves due to their intensive usage of cache. We plan to address this issue in our future work. One way to alleviate this shortcoming is to launch placeholder kernels from the host-side service to occupy a subset of SMs and force the GPU block scheduler to assign thread blocks to the free SMs. The overhead associated with this approach is expected to be minimal, since the placeholder kernels are only required for the short period of time between arriving a kernel launch request at the host-side service and the launch of the kernel at the GPU.

There are other limitations imposed by the choice of platform. One is due to the use of MPS in our system. NVIDIA GPUs do not support dynamic parallelism [13] while running MPS. Therefore, our system does not support running the kernels that use this feature. The other, perhaps more important limitation, is that NVIDIA GPUs prior to the Volta [20] do not support running kernels with separate virtual address spaces, which creates security concerns. As discussed earlier in the paper, adding a software address translation layer [25] can solve this problem by isolating the address spaces of different applications.

## 4   Evaluation

In this section, we first describe the platform for our experiments. Then we discuss the characteristics of the benchmark kernels we used. After that, the effect of the transformation in Sect. 3.4 on the performance of the benchmark kernels is evaluated. Finally, we present results for multi-kernel evaluations.

### 4.1   Platform

The machine we used for the experiments has an Intel Xeon E5-2640 CPU, and the experiments are conducted on an NVIDIA Tesla K40c GPU. The OS is Ubuntu 16.04, and NVIDIA driver version 375.26 and CUDA 8.0 were used to compile and run benchmarks. Table 2 shows the specifications of the GPU card accounted for while making decisions about feasibility of kernel configurations in the host-side service.

**Table 2.** NVIDIA Tesla K40c specifications.

| Resource | Value |
| --- | --- |
| Threads per SM | 2048 |
| Registers per SM | 65536 |
| Shared Memory per SM | 48 KB |
| Warps per SM | 64 |
| Thread Blocks per SM | 16 |

## 4.2    Benchmark Kernels

Our goal was to have a mixture of kernels from various areas with different behaviors and requirements. To this end, we picked seven benchmark kernels, binomialOptions, FDTD3d, lavaMD, MD5hash, nbody, particlefilter, and tpacf, from CUDA SDK samples [16], Rodinia [5], SHOC [7], and Parboil [26] benchmark suites, for our evaluations. Figure 7 shows the behavior of these benchmarks that are representative of a variety of kernels. The values on the axes are from a scale of 0–10 and are obtained from NVIDIA profiler. The figure shows that some kernels are compute-intensive (MD5Hash, lavaMD), some demonstrate intensive use of memory and cache (FDTD3d), and some have a mixture of requirements (binomialOptions, nbody, particlefilter, tpacf).

Table 3 summarizes the characteristics of these benchmark kernels, after undergoing the transformations to support adaptive simultaneous multi-tenancy explained in Sect. 3.4. The abbreviations in front of kernels' names are used in multi-kernel evaluation figures.

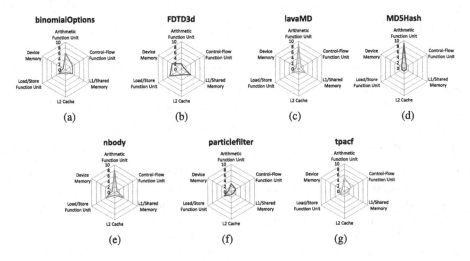

**Fig. 7.** Utilization of various resource types in (a) binomialOptions, (b) FDTD3d, (c) lavaMD, (d) MD5Hash, (e) nbody, (f) particlefilter, and (g) tpacf kernels.

## 4.3    Single Kernel Performance

Figure 8a shows the normalized execution time of the transformed kernels with respect to the original code. As the figure illustrates, applying the transformation to the kernels has a negligible impact of 1.7% on the average performance of all kernels. However, it increases the register and shared memory usage of the kernels due to introducing additional variables. The register usage is increased by 23%, as shown in Fig. 8b. Increasing the number of registers per thread might result in

**Table 3.** Benchmark kernels characteristics.

| Kernel | Thread blocks | Threads / Block | Registers / Thread | Shared memory/ Block (B) | Execution time (ms) | ISU |
|---|---|---|---|---|---|---|
| binomialOptions (BO) [16] | 1024 | 128 | 28 | 524 | 5.476 | 73.6 |
| FDTD3d (FD) [16] | 288 | 512 | 58 | 3848 | 8.821 | 27.5 |
| lavaMD (LM) [5] | 512 | 128 | 64 | 7208 | 8.958 | 87.3 |
| MD5Hash (MD) [7] | 25432 | 384 | 30 | 8 | 71.475 | 97.4 |
| nbody (NB) [16] | 128 | 256 | 49 | 8208 | 39.155 | 89.1 |
| particlefilter (PF) [5] | 512 | 128 | 16 | 8 | 43.105 | 48.6 |
| tpacf (TP) [26] | 201 | 256 | 49 | 13320 | 11.23 | 34.8 |

fewer CTAs fitting on the GPU. Nevertheless, as shown in Fig. 9, increasing the number of CTAs has marginal gain and after some point, the performance does not improve dramatically by increasing the number of CTAs. Anyway, a possible solution for reducing the register overhead of the proposed code transformations is to restrict the compiler to compile kernels with fewer registers. This incurs some performance overhead to kernels, but based on our observations accepting a 2% performance overhead results in the elimination of register usage overhead. The reason that we did not take this into consideration is that the same could be applied to the original kernels for register reduction. Thus, we picked the best-performing register configuration for both original and transformed kernels. We did not include the shared memory usage figures, because all kernels need a fixed eight bytes additional shared memory to store the logical block index and CTA IDs in SMs required for the persistent threads transformation.

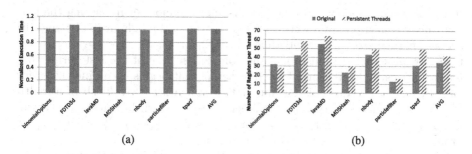

(a)                                                (b)

**Fig. 8.** (a) Performance and (b) register usage of benchmark kernels under persistent threads transformation.

As stated in Sect. 3.4, applying persistent threads transformation to kernels allows to control the allocated resources by running them with the desired number of CTAs. Figure 9 shows the performance of transformed kernels for varying numbers of CTAs per SM. We use these data as input for our greedy allocation algorithm. Most of the time, there is a direct trade-off between the numbers

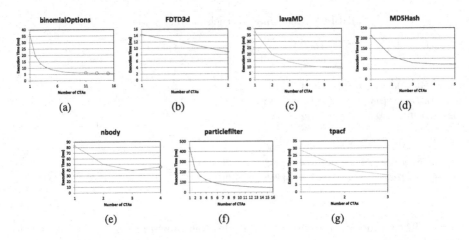

**Fig. 9.** Performance of (a) binomialOptions, (b) FDTD3d, (c) lavaMD, (d) MD5Hash, (e) nbody, (f) particlefilter, and (g) tpacf kernels with different numbers of CTAs.

of CTAs of a kernel and its performance. However, there are some exceptions for binomialOptions and nbody that are distinguished with red dotted circles. We omit these points from the decision-making process in the allocation algorithm, since they do not offer any beneficial trade-off. In other words, there exists another point in the space that uses less resources but delivers higher performance.

## 4.4   Multi-kernel Performance

In this section, we report two metrics that are common for measuring the performance of multi-program workloads [8]: (i) system throughput (STP), and (ii) average normalized turnaround time (ANTT) for kernels. We use the time it takes for all kernels to finish, i.e., the completion time of the last kernel that finishes minus the start time of the first kernel that begins, as an indication for STP. ANTT is the ratio of the time it takes for a kernel to finish in a multi-tenant environment and the time it takes for the same kernel to finish in isolation. Unfortunately, we cannot report ISU for multi-kernel experiments since NVIDIA profiler does not report it when MPS is running.

We also report results for two systems: (i) a system in which there is no host-side service, but persistent thread transformation is applied to kernels (PT), and (ii) our proposed adaptive simultaneous multi-tenant system (SiM).

We repeated our experiments five times for every ordering of the kernels (e.g., for combination of BO+FD, five times when BO arrived at the service first, five times when FD was the first, and for SiM only, five times when both arrived at almost the same time such that their effects were aggregated), and report the average of the results.

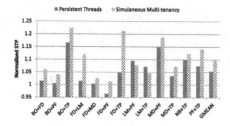

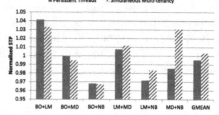

**Fig. 10.** Normalized STP under different combinations of kernels including at least one kernel with low ISU.

**Fig. 11.** Normalized STP under different combinations of kernels with high ISUs.

**Kernels with Low ISU.** We refer to kernels with an ISU of less than 50% as low ISU kernels. During the execution of such kernels, execution units are idles for more than half of the cycles due to various reasons, including synchronization, data request, execution dependency, busy pipeline, etc. It is expected that co-scheduling these kernels with another kernel results in higher STP, since the idle cycles can be taken advantage of. Figure 10 demonstrates the normalized STP for kernel combinations that include at least one kernel with low ISU. On average, PT improves STP by 5.3% with respect to the sequential execution of kernels. This improvement is due to the alleviation of the head-of-line blocking at the GPU block scheduler explained in Sect. 2.4. Nevertheless, addressing this issue alone is not sufficient to realize the potential STP improvement created by the underutilization of resources. To this end, by tuning the resources allocated to each kernel, SiM increases STP by 9.8%.

Not all kernel pairs experience similar improvements in STP. The higher the ISU of one of the kernels is, the less opportunities there are for STP improvement. This is evident in FD+MD and MD+TP pairs, because MD kernel has an ISU of 97.4%. This basically means that MD alone can utilize the device very well. There are other factors that impact the achieved STP improvement as well, such as the resource requirement of the kernels, the execution time of a single thread block of the kernels, and non-optimal allocation of resources by our greedy algorithm. The first one shows itself in high STPs achieved when running BO+TP and FD+TP pairs, since these kernels utilize different units on the device. The other two, however, explain the low STP improvement for LM+TP. In this kernel pair, whenever LM arrives first, there is no room for TP to run any thread blocks until the first round of thread blocks of LM are completed and preemption can take place. This takes long enough to offset a large enough fraction of the improvement achieved by the co-run of the rest of the thread blocks of the two kernels to cause lower improvements than simply running the two kernels with persistent thread transformation. In addition, the launch parameters determined by the greedy algorithm for the two kernels do not result in the best possible output. This highlights the need for a more accurate and sophisticated allocation policy, which is part of our future work.

The gains in STP come at the expense of 49.2% increase in ANTT. We must note that improving STP and keeping ANTT low are at odds with each other, and the goal of our allocation policy is to maximize STP. If ANTT is an important factor in the system, other allocation algorithms can replace our greedy algorithm without affecting other parts of the system. Besides, we did not define priorities for kernels in our work. The works that target improving ANTT, do so for high priority kernels since it is impossible to improve this metric for all kernels in the system.

**Kernels with High ISU.** The STP improvement is not significant when all the kernels running on the GPU can utilize it well enough when executed in isolation. Figure 11 shows the normalized STP for pairs of kernels that both have high ISUs (i.e., greater that 50%). In these cases, the overheads of preemption and multiple launches, as well as cache thrashing, result in a negligible STP improvement of 0.3% in SiM. PT even imposes a 0.5% overhead on STP. The other downside of running high-ISU kernels together is a large increase in ANTT (78.7%).

These observations mean that adaptive simultaneous multi-tenancy is more effective when individual kernels are not highly optimized to have high ISUs. The positive side is that this also means that without putting extra effort for optimizing kernels, a higher STP can be achieved by merely running multiple kernels together.

## 5    Related Work

### 5.1    Persistent Threads

Gupta et al. studied the different use cases of persistent threads for a single kernel [11]. Recently, in independent works, Chen et al. [6] and Wu et al. [30] proposed taking advantage of persistent threads for supporting preemption. EffiSha [6] only supports execution of one kernel at any given time on the GPU. FLEP [30], on the other hand, has limited support for executing two kernels on the GPU at the same time, only in the case that one of the kernels is small enough to entirely fit on the GPU. Supporting preemption in these works helps favoring the high priority kernels over the low priority ones, but it does not solve the underutilization of resources on the device.

### 5.2    Software-Based Multi-tasking on GPUs

Pai et al. proposed Elastic Kernels [21] and showed that sharing the GPU among multiple kernels improves utilization. They artificially fuse multiple kernels together to form a super-kernel in a single GPU context. There are other works that adopt a similar approach [10,14,29]. This allows for concurrent execution of kernels, but such a scenario is impractical in the real world, since merging the kernels from different clients into a single kernel at run-time is impossible. We avoid this limitation by using a host-side service and taking advantage of MPS. Furthermore, the focus of this paper and [21] is on different parts of the solution. We propose a system to solve the problem of multi-tenancy while [21] proposes various policies that can be employed in our host-side service.

Preemptive Kernel Model [3] proposed by Basaran and Kang slices the kernel into smaller grids which in turn allows for sharing the GPU among multiple kernels. Several other works also rely on kernel slicing [12,32]. This approach incurs the overhead of multiple launches that cannot be avoided even if we do not need to preempt the kernel at all. By taking advantage of persistent threads model, our approach eliminates the unnecessary launch overhead introduced by kernel slicing.

### 5.3    Hardware-Based Multi-tasking on GPUs

The NVIDIA Volta architecture supports static simultaneous multi-tenancy [20]. In other words, it is possible to divide the GPU into multiple smaller virtual GPUs. There are also works that introduce hardware extensions to support preemption or multi-programming. Tanasic et al. [27] proposed context switching and draining by supporting preemption in hardware. Park et al. [22] extended this work by identifying idempotent kernels to faster preempt the running kernel by flushing the SMs.

Adriaens et al proposed spatial multi-tasking [1]. In this approach, each SM is entirely allocated to one kernel. Wang et al. propose partial context switching (PCS) [28], which is similar to our approach in that it only preempts a portion of SMs. Nevertheless, they use different allocation policies and hardware support is necessary for its implementation. Xu et al. [31] propose a software-hardware mechanism that similarly shares an SM among multiple kernels. Park et al. propose GPU Maestro [23] that based on performance predictions switches between spatial multi-tasking and PCS at run-time.

These works address the issues regarding supporting multi-tenancy on GPUs, but because of the required hardware modifications are not applicable to the existing devices. Our goal in this paper is to design a system that can take advantage of commodity GPUs.

## 6    Conclusion

In this paper, we identify the challenges of using GPUs in a multi-tenant environment. We propose adaptive simultaneous multi-tenancy for GPUs to overcome these challenges. Our approach comprises a host-side service that makes decisions about the kernel launch parameters and when the kernels should preempt. We also provide an API to facilitate using the system for programmers and allowing kernels to dynamically adapt resource usage at runtime and require minimal kernel modifications. Evaluation of our prototype system on NVIDIA K40c GPUs show that, on average, system throughput is improved by 9.8% for combinations of kernels that include at least one low-utilization kernel. This improvement is achieved at the cost of 49.2% increase in average normalized turn around time. Combinations of high-utilization kernels do not benefit from our system. Our observations indicate that using adaptive simultaneous multi-tenancy allows programmers to avoid highly optimizing their kernels to have high ISUs by providing higher STP for concurrent execution of low-utilization kernels.

As future work, we plan to investigate the effectiveness of more sophisticated mapping mechanisms and allocation policies to support asymmetric mapping of thread blocks to SMs. This way, cache-intensive kernels can benefit from having the entire L1 cache to themselves. We also plan to exploit various scheduling algorithms for dispatching thread blocks to SMs, to improve locality and reduce destructive interference in L2 cache.

**Acknowledgments.** This work is supported in part by the National Science Foundation (CCF-1335443) and equipment donations from NVIDIA.

# References

1. Adriaens, J.T., Compton, K., Kim, N.S., Schulte, M.J.: The case for GPGPU spatial multitasking. In: Proceedings of the 2012 IEEE 18th International Symposium on High-Performance Computer Architecture. HPCA 2012, pp. 1–12. IEEE Computer Society, Washington, DC (2012). http://dx.doi.org/10.1109/HPCA.2012.6168946
2. Amazon Web Services: Elastic GPUS (2017). https://aws.amazon.com/ec2/Elastic-GPUs/
3. Basaran, C., Kang, K.D.: Supporting preemptive task executions and memory copies in GPGPUS. In: Proceedings of the 2012 24th Euromicro Conference on Real-Time Systems. ECRTS 2012, pp. 287–296. IEEE Computer Society, Washington, DC (2012). http://dx.doi.org/10.1109/ECRTS.2012.15
4. Chase, J.S., Anderson, D.C., Thakar, P.N., Vahdat, A.M., Doyle, R.P.: Managing energy and server resources in hosting centers. In: Proceedings of the Eighteenth ACM Symposium on Operating Systems Principles. SOSP 2001, pp. 103–116. ACM, New York (2001). http://doi.acm.org/10.1145/502034.502045
5. Che, S., Sheaffer, J.W., Boyer, M., Szafaryn, L.G., Wang, L., Skadron, K.: A characterization of the Rodinia benchmark suite with comparison to contemporary cmp workloads. In: Proceedings of the IEEE International Symposium on Workload Characterization (IISWC 2010), pp. 1–11. IISWC 2010. IEEE Computer Society, Washington, DC (2010). http://dx.doi.org/10.1109/IISWC.2010.5650274
6. Chen, G., Zhao, Y., Shen, X., Zhou, H.: Effisha: a software framework for enabling effficient preemptive scheduling of GPU. In: Proceedings of the 22Nd ACM SIGPLAN Symposium on Principles and Practice of Parallel Programming, pp. 3–16. PPoPP 2017, ACM, New York (2017). http://doi.acm.org/10.1145/3018743.3018748
7. Danalis, A., et al.: The scalable heterogeneous computing (shoc) benchmark suite. In: Proceedings of the 3rd Workshop on General-Purpose Computation on Graphics Processing Units, pp. 63–74. GPGPU-3, ACM, New York (2010). http://doi.acm.org/10.1145/1735688.1735702
8. Eyerman, S., Eeckhout, L.: System-level performance metrics for multiprogram workloads. IEEE Micro **28**(3), 42–53 (2008)
9. Google: Google cloud platforms (2017). https://cloud.google.com/gpu/
10. Gregg, C., Dorn, J., Hazelwood, K., Skadron, K.: Fine-grained Resource Sharing for Concurrent GPGPU Kernels. In: Proceedings of the 4th USENIX Conference on Hot Topics in Parallelism. HotPar 2012, p. 10. USENIX Association, Berkeley, (2012). http://dl.acm.org/citation.cfm?id=2342788.2342798

11. Gupta, K., Stuart, J.A., Owens, J.D.: A study of persistent threads style GPU programming for GPGPU workloads. In: 2012 Innovative Parallel Computing (InPar), pp. 1–14, May 2012
12. Jiao, Q., Lu, M., Huynh, H.P., Mitra, T.: Improving GPGPU energy-efficiency through concurrent kernel execution and DVFs. In: Proceedings of the 13th Annual IEEE/ACM International Symposium on Code Generation and Optimization. CGO 2015, pp. 1–11. IEEE Computer Society, Washington, DC (2015). http://dl.acm.org/citation.cfm?id=2738600.2738602
13. Jones, S.: Introduction to dynamic parallelism. In: Nvidia GPU Technology Conference. NVIDIA (2012). http://developer.download.nvidia.com/GTC/PDF/GTC2012/PresentationPDF/S0338-GTC2012-CUDA-Programming-Model.pdf
14. Liang, Y., Huynh, H.P., Rupnow, K., Goh, R.S.M., Chen, D.: Efficient gpu spatial-temporal multitasking. IEEE Trans. Parall. Distrib. Syst. **26**(3), 748–760 (2015)
15. Microsoft: Microsoft azure (2016). https://azure.microsoft.com/en-us/blog/azure-n-series-general-availability-on-december-1/
16. Nvidia: CUDA programming guide (2008). https://docs.nvidia.com/cuda/cuda-c-programming-guide/
17. Nvidia: Next generation CUDA computer architecture Kepler GK110 (2012)
18. NVIDIA: Multi-process service (2015). https://docs.nvidia.com/deploy/pdf/CUDA_Multi_Process_Service_Overview.pdf
19. NVIDIA: Pascal architecture whitepaper, June 2015. http://www.nvidia.com/object/pascal-architecture-whitepaper.html
20. NVIDIA: Volta architecture whitepaper, June 2015. http://www.nvidia.com/object/volta-architecture-whitepaper.html
21. Pai, S., Thazhuthaveetil, M.J., Govindarajan, R.: Improving GPGPU concurrency with elastic kernels. In: Proceedings of the Eighteenth International Conference on Architectural Support for Programming Languages and Operating Systems, pp. 407–418. ASPLOS 2013, ACM, New York (2013). http://doi.acm.org/10.1145/2451116.2451160
22. Park, J.J.K., Park, Y., Mahlke, S.: Chimera: collaborative preemption for multitasking on a shared GPU. In: Proceedings of the Twentieth International Conference on Architectural Support for Programming Languages and Operating Systems. ASPLOS 2015, pp. 593–606. ACM, New York (2015). http://doi.acm.org/10.1145/2694344.2694346
23. Park, J.J.K., Park, Y., Mahlke, S.: Dynamic resource management for efficient utilization of multitasking GPUs. In: Proceedings of the Twenty-Second International Conference on Architectural Support for Programming Languages and Operating Systems. ASPLOS 2017, pp. 527–540. ACM, New York (2017). http://doi.acm.org/10.1145/3037697.3037707
24. Randles, M., Lamb, D., Taleb-Bendiab, A.: A comparative study into distributed load balancing algorithms for cloud computing. In: 2010 IEEE 24th International Conference on Advanced Information Networking and Applications Workshops, pp. 551–556, April 2010
25. Shahar, S., Bergman, S., Silberstein, M.: Activepointers: a case for software address translation on GPUs. In: Proceedings of the 43rd International Symposium on Computer Architecture. ISCA 2016, pp. 596–608. IEEE Press, Piscataway (2016). https://doi.org/10.1109/ISCA.2016.58
26. Stratton, J.A., et al.: Parboil: a revised benchmark suite for scientific and commercial throughput computing. Technical report (2012). https://scholar.google.com/scholar?oi=bibs&hl=en&cluster=14097255143770688510

27. Tanasic, I., Gelado, I., Cabezas, J., Ramirez, A., Navarro, N., Valero, M.: Enabling preemptive multiprogramming on GPUs. In: Proceeding of the 41st Annual International Symposium on Computer Architecuture, pp. 193–204. ISCA 2014, IEEE Press, Piscataway (2014). http://dl.acm.org/citation.cfm?id=2665671.2665702

28. Wang, Z., Yang, J., Melhem, R., Childers, B., Zhang, Y., Guo, M.: Simultaneous multikernel GPU: Multi-tasking throughput processors via fine-grained sharing. In: 2016 IEEE International Symposium on High Performance Computer Architecture (HPCA), pp. 358–369, March 2016

29. Wu, B., Chen, G., Li, D., Shen, X., Vetter, J.: Enabling and exploiting flexible task assignment on GPU through SM-centric program transformations. In: Proceedings of the 29th ACM on International Conference on Supercomputing. ICS 2015, pp. 119–130. ACM, New York (2015). http://doi.acm.org/10.1145/2751205.2751213

30. Wu, B., Liu, X., Zhou, X., Jiang, C.: Flep: enabling flexible and efficient preemption on GPUs. In: Proceedings of the Twenty-Second International Conference on Architectural Support for Programming Languages and Operating Systems, pp. 483–496. ASPLOS 2017, ACM, New York (2017). http://doi.acm.org/10.1145/3037697.3037742

31. Xu, Q., Jeon, H., Kim, K., Ro, W.W., Annavaram, M.: Warped-slicer: Efficient intra-SM slicing through dynamic resource partitioning for GPU multiprogramming. In: 2016 ACM/IEEE 43rd Annual International Symposium on Computer Architecture (ISCA), pp. 230–242, June 2016

32. Zhong, J., He, B.: Kernelet: high-throughput gpu kernel executions with dynamic slicing and scheduling. IEEE Trans. Parallel Distrib. Syst. **25**(6), 1522–1532 (2014). https://doi.org/10.1109/TPDS.2013.257

# Stochastic Programming Approach for Resource Selection Under Demand Uncertainty

Tanveer Hossain Bhuiyan[1], Mahantesh Halappanavar[2]([⊠]), Ryan D. Friese[2], Hugh Medal[1], Luis de la Torre[3], Arun Sathanur[2], and Nathan R. Tallent[2]

[1] Mississippi State University, Starkville, USA
tb2038@msstate.edu,hmedal@ise.msstate.edu
[2] Pacific Northwest National Laboratory, Richland, USA
{Mahantesh.Halappanavar,Ryan.Friese,
Arun.Sathanur,Nathan.Tallent}@pnnl.gov
[3] Washington State University, Pullman, USA
luis.delatorre@wsu.edu

**Abstract.** Cost-efficient selection and scheduling of a subset of geographically distributed resources to meet the demands of a scientific workflow is a challenging problem. The problem is exacerbated by uncertainties in demand and availability of resources. In this paper, we present a stochastic optimization based framework for robust decision making in the selection of distributed resources over a planning horizon under demand uncertainty. We present a novel two-stage stochastic programming model for resource selection, and implement an L-shaped decomposition algorithm to solve this model. A Sample Average Approximation algorithm is integrated to enable stochastic optimization to solve problems with a large number of scenarios. Using the metric of stochastic solution, we demonstrate up to **30%** cost reduction relative to solutions without explicit consideration of demand uncertainty for a 24-month problem. We also demonstrate up to **54%** cost reduction relative to a previously developed solution for a 36-month problem. We further argue that the composition of resources selected is superior to solutions computed without explicit consideration of uncertainties. Given the importance of resource selection and scheduling of complex scientific workflows, especially in the context of commercial cloud computing, we believe that our novel stochastic programming framework will benefit many researchers as well as users of distributed computing resources.

## 1 Introduction

Scheduling of large-scale scientific workflows on geographically distributed resources is a challenging problem. Optimal selection of a subset of available resources to meet the projected demand is usually the first step in scheduling. Given a wide range of resources, from dedicated high-performance clusters to

© Springer Nature Switzerland AG 2019
D. Klusáček et al. (Eds.): JSSPP 2018, LNCS 11332, pp. 107–126, 2019.
https://doi.org/10.1007/978-3-030-10632-4_6

commercial cloud computing platforms, that are available to a scientific work-flow, cost-efficient selection of resources is a challenging problem. Further, uncertainties not only in demand but also in the availability of resources exacerbates the problem. To address this problem, we present a stochastic programming based approach in this paper. Our goal is to compute cost-efficient selection of resources under demand uncertainties. We build on our prior work [6], where we introduced the problem of resource selection under demand uncertainties. Here, we develop a stochastic programming based framework that significantly improves the quality of solutions.

Our study is motivated by complex workflows from the Belle II experiments, a high energy physics experiment to probe the interactions of fundamental constituents of our universe [9]. Computing and storage resources to support the Belle II experiments span several continents with users across the globe. Data is generated both from the Belle II detector and Monte Carlo simulations, and is expected to reach 350 peta bytes (a peta byte is $10^{15}$ bytes) by the end of the experiment in 2022. Complex workflows run across multiple computing and storage resources distributed worldwide. Multiple research and commercial cloud computing resources are also used. With a wide variety of user jobs and resource types, the Belle II experiment is an ideal case study to develop efficient solutions for scheduling of complex workflows.

Inspired by a resource selection problem in electric power grids, we model our problem as a *unit commitment* problem, where the goal is to meet a forecasted demand with a subset of resources at a minimum cost [8]. We describe the problem in Sect. 2. We then introduce the notion of uncertainties in demand, where the forecasted demand varies due to several factors. This formulation enables us to propose a *two-stage mixed-integer stochastic program* as an efficient solution technique. We detail the mathematical formulation in Sect. 3. Intuitively, stochastic programming is a mathematical programming technique for modeling optimization problems that involve uncertainties [3]. Stochastic programming can exploit the fact that probability distributions governing the data are known or can be estimated. For workflows with demand uncertainties, our goal is to develop a large set of scenarios of the forecasted demand, drawn from known probability distributions. Stochastic programming will compute solutions that are feasible for all scenarios and maximizes the expectation of an objective function. In the two-stage model, we make a resource selection decision in the first stage, after which each realization of the demand (a scenario) is considered that affects the outcome of the first-stage decision. A penalty is added for any unsatisfied demand from the second-stage, and the first-stage problem is adjusted accordingly. We employ the *Sample Average Approximation* (SAA) method as a sampling strategy to improve computational complexity, and use an *L-shaped decomposition algorithm* within the SAA procedure to solve the mixed-integer stochastic programming problem. We detail this approach in Sect. 4.

Using a carefully designed synthetic workflow inspired from the Belle II experiment, we present experimental evaluation of the proposed solution in Sect. 6. We demonstrate the superior quality of the proposed solution not only with respect to the previously developed method, but also with optimal solutions that are computed without explicit consideration of demand uncertainties. We demonstrate up to **30%** cost reduction relative to solutions without explicit consideration of uncertainty for a 24-month use case, and up to **54%** cost reduction relative to a Genetic Algorithm based solution for a 36-month use case. We further argue that the proposed solution method leads to resource compositions that are superior and robust to price fluctuations. To the best of our knowledge, this is the first detailed work on employing stochastic programming approach for scheduling of complex workflows with demand uncertainties.

We make the following contributions in this paper:

- Develop a novel two-stage stochastic programming model for the allocation of distributed resources over a long range planning horizon with demand uncertainties to minimize the total expected cost.
- Implement and evaluate a stochastic optimization algorithm (L-shaped decomposition algorithm) to efficiently solve the proposed optimization problem.
- Integrate Sample Average Approximation method with the L-shaped decomposition algorithm to solve problems with continuous distribution of demand uncertainties with a large number of scenarios.
- Present numerical results to demonstrate the benefit of considering uncertainty in resource selection relative to a deterministic approach considering only the base demands (without uncertainty) in decision making.
- Present numerical results to demonstrate the robustness of the solution computed using a stochastic optimization approach relative to existing approaches.

## 2    Problem Description

Given a set of diverse computing resources with varying costs of usage, the objective is to compute the most cost-efficient subset of resources to meet the forecasted demand. This problem is analogous to the *unit commitment* problem in the context of electric power grid [19]. Unit commitment is a resource utilization problem where the objective is to select a subset of power generators at a minimum cost to satisfy a given demand that varies over time. Different power generators have different start-up and operation costs. Mathematically, the unit commitment problem can be formulated as shown in Eq. 1, where, $f$ is the total cost of the system for $N$ power generators chosen to satisfy the demand over the planning horizon $T$. Variables $S_j$ and $C_j$ are the start-up and operating cost for each generator $j$ respectively, to generate $P_j$ units of power. The binary variable $x_{jt}$ represents whether the generator $j$ is on or off at time period $t$. The system also specifies a reserved demand, $R_t$, for every time period that is satisfied by the spinning reserve (spare capacity), $r_t$.

$$min \ f = \sum_{t=1}^{T} \sum_{j=1}^{N} (S_j x_{jt} + C_j P_{jt}) \qquad (1a)$$

$$s.t. \ \sum_{j=1}^{N} P_{jt} \geq D_t \qquad \forall t = 1,..,T \qquad (1b)$$

$$\sum_{j=1}^{N} r_{jt} \geq R_t \qquad \forall t = 1,..,T. \qquad (1c)$$

In this paper, we introduce a similar resource utilization problem in the context of large-scale workflows, where we need to allocate geographically distributed computing resources to satisfy the demand over a planning horizon. The selection problem is pronounced in the context of cloud computing where different types of resources are available with varying cost structures. For example, Amazon EC2 offers several types of resources with different fixed (subscription) and usage (operating) costs (detailed in Sect. 5). Using a computing resource incurs two types of costs: A subscription cost and an operating cost. A resource can only be used within a given period that it has been subscribed for. There are three broad types of machine usage policies: Total-upfront, partial-upfront (hybrid), and on-demand. In total-upfront, a machine is subscribed or paid upfront for a contiguous block of time without an operating cost for its use. In partial-upfront, a machine is also subscribed for several contiguous time periods, but incur an operating cost for using the machine during those periods. On-demand machines do not require any subscription cost, but incur higher operating costs when used. We also assume a penalty cost for any unmet demand for a given period that can be considered as *spot pricing* in the cloud computing literature.

Our objective is to compute the minimum-cost allocation of resources to satisfy forecasted demands under uncertainty. The demand fluctuates significantly over a planing horizon relative to the forecasted baseline. Demand fluctuations are addressed in unit commitment through reserves, $r_t$. However, estimating and maintaining spare capacity at every time period is an expensive solution. We therefore develop a stochastic programming approach to address this problem. We will describe our approach in the following section.

## 3    Two-Stage Stochastic Programming Model

We formulate the resource selection problem under demand uncertainty as a two-stage mixed-integer stochastic programming model. In order to address uncertainties in demand, which can arise from several factors such as errors in planning and unforeseen circumstances, we construct specific demand scenarios by sampling from a continuous distribution of base demands over the horizon with estimated probability distribution functions (Sect. 4.1).

Each scenario represents a particular demand curve spanning the entire horizon. In the first stage of the two-stage programming model, subscription decisions are made before realizing the uncertainty. In other words, the machines are subscribed at the beginning of the planning horizon when the actual demand for each period is unknown to the decision maker. In contrast to the first-stage problem, the second-stage problem considers the uncertainties, where the decisions are made as to whether to use or not to use a machine that has already been subscribed for a given period of time. Feedback from the second-stage problem is used to improve the decision making in the first-stage problem. Our objective is to minimize the total subscription cost as well as the expected operating costs while satisfying the demand under uncertainties over the planning horizon, where $\omega$ is the set of random scenarios. We detail the mathematical formulation in this section. Notations used in this paper are summarized in Table 1.

$$min \; f(x) = \sum_{t=1}^{T}\sum_{j=1}^{N} S_j x_{jt} + E[Q(x,\omega)] \qquad (2a)$$

$$s.t. \qquad \sum_{t'=t}^{min\{T,t+(u1-1)\}} x_{jt'} \le 1 \qquad \forall j \in J_{NS1}, \forall t = 1,..,T \qquad (2b)$$

$$\sum_{t'=t}^{min\{T,t+(u2-1)\}} x_{jt'} \le 1 \qquad \forall j \in J_{NS2}, \forall t = 1,..,T \qquad (2c)$$

$$x_{jt} \in \{0,1\} \qquad \forall j \in J, \forall t = 1,..,T \qquad (2d)$$

$$Q(\hat{x},\omega) = min \sum_{t=1}^{T}\sum_{j=1}^{N} C_j p_{jt}^{\omega} + \sum_{t=1}^{T} \lambda l_t^{\omega} \qquad (3a)$$

$$s.t. \qquad \sum_{j=1}^{N} P_j(p_{jt}^{\omega}) + l_t^{\omega} \ge d_t^{\omega} \qquad \forall t = 1,..,T \qquad (3b)$$

$$P_{jt}^{\omega} \le \hat{x}_{jt} \qquad \forall j \in J_{OND}, \forall t = 1,...,T \qquad (3c)$$

$$P_{jt}^{\omega} \le \sum_{t'=max\{1,t-(u1-1)\}}^{t} \hat{x}_{jt'} \qquad \forall j \in J_{NS1}, \forall t = 1,..,T \qquad (3d)$$

$$P_{jt}^{\omega} \le \sum_{t'=max\{1,t-(u2-1)\}}^{t} \hat{x}_{jt'} \qquad \forall j \in J_{NS2}, \forall t = 1,..,T \qquad (3e)$$

$$0 \le P_{jt}^{\omega} \le 1 \qquad \forall j \in J, \forall t = 1,..,T \qquad (3f)$$

The two-stage stochastic programming problem is formulated as follows. The objective function, Eq. 2a, of the first-stage model is to subscribe (select) a set of machines for the entire planning horizon, such that the total subscription cost and the expected total operating cost are simultaneously minimized across all the scenarios. Constraints 2b and 2c ensure that if a machine is subscribed at a period $t$ for $p$ number of periods, the subscription costs are incurred only once. Constraint 2d models the binary nature of the subscription decision

**Table 1.** A summary of the notations used in this paper.

| Notation | Description |
|----------|-------------|
| **Sets** | |
| $J$ | Set of machines, $j \in J$ |
| $J_{OND}$ | On-demand machines |
| $J_{NS1}$ | 12 month-subscription machines |
| $J_{NS2}$ | 36 month-subscription machines |
| **Parameters** | |
| $u$ | No. of periods for which machine $j$ is subscribed |
| $N$ | No. of machines |
| $d_t^\omega$ | Demand at period $t$ in scenario $\omega \in \Omega$ |
| $S_j$ | Subscription cost for machine $j$ |
| $C_j$ | Operating cost of machine $j$ for a single period |
| $T$ | Total planning horizon |
| $\lambda$ | Penalty cost for unsatisfied demand |
| $P_j$ | Computing power of machine $j$ |
| **Variables** | |
| $x_{jt}$ | 1 if machine $j$ is subscribed at period $t$, 0 otherwise |
| $p_{jt}^\omega$ | Fraction of period $t$ machine $j$ is used in scenario $\omega$ |
| $l_t^\omega$ | Computing power shortage in period $t$ in scenario $\omega$ |

variables. The second-stage model stands for each realization of a randomly sampled demand scenario.

The objective function, Eq. 3a, of the second-stage model minimizes the total operating cost over all periods for a given scenario. A penalty is added to the objective function for any unsatisfied demand. The objective function has two components. The first component computes the total operating cost of machines over the planning horizon $T$, and the second component computes the total penalty cost for unmet demand across $T$. Constraint 3b represents the demand to be satisfied for each time period. A variable is introduced to satisfy the shortage in demand. Constraint 3c imposes the subscription requirement to use on-demand machines. In order to use a total-upfront or partial-upfront machine $j$ for period $t$, that period should be within the range of periods $p$ for which the machine has been subscribed in the first-stage model. This requirement is satisfied for machines with 12 months and 36 months subscription periods in Constraints 3d and 3e, respectively. Constraint 3f represents the bounds for usage of machines. We present an approach to efficiently solve the two-stage stochastic programming model in Sect. 4.

# 4 Solution Approaches

We now present our solution to the two-stage stochastic programming model described in Sect. 3. A particular challenge in the solution of this problem arises due to the difficulty in computing the expected operating cost in the first-stage objective function, 2a. For a given first-stage solution, we need to compute the expected operating cost over all the realizations of the uncertain demand. If we consider the distribution of the uncertain demand to be continuous for each period, the computation of the expected operating cost requires taking multiple integrals, which will be computationally challenging [18]. On the other hand, if we consider the demand distribution to be discrete, we will have a large number of scenarios (realizations) to consider. For example, consider a 36-month problem. If the demand for each period has 10 different discrete values, the total number of possible scenarios to be considered will be $10^{36}$. Thus, the challenge will be to compute a large number of scenarios, and consequently, solve a large number of linear programming problems corresponding to these scenarios which is computationally infeasible.

To reduce the computational complexity in solving the two-stage stochastic program with infinitely many scenarios, we implement a sampling strategy called the Sample Average Approximation (SAA) [15,20]. SAA enables the solution of stochastic allocation problem with continuous distributions for demand uncertainties. We integrate SAA with the L-shaped decomposition algorithm [1,21] to solve the two-stage problem efficiently. This approach is motivated by the success of our own work [2] and of other researchers [18] to solve similar problems in different domains. We briefly describe the integrated approach in this section.

## 4.1 Sample Average Approximation

We use Sample Average Approximation (SAA) to deal with the difficulty in computing the expectation in the objective function 2a. SAA approximates the expected cost component, $E[Q(x,\omega)]$, of the objective function by a sample average function, $\frac{1}{|\Omega|}\sum_{s=1}^{|\Omega|} Q(x,\omega^s)$. SAA generates a set of random samples $(\omega^1, \omega^2, ..., \omega^{|\Omega|})$ of size $|\Omega|$, where $\Omega$ is the set of scenarios (realizations) indexed by $\omega$. Thus, the original problem in Eq. 2 is approximated as:

$$min_{x \in X} \hat{f}(x) := \sum_{t=1}^{T}\sum_{j=1}^{N} S_j x_{jt} + \frac{1}{|\Omega|}\sum_{s=1}^{|\Omega|} Q(x,\omega^s). \tag{4}$$

We denote the optimal solution and optimal objective value of the approximation problem (Eq. 4) by $\hat{x}$ and $V$, respectively. Here, $\hat{x}$ and $V$ are stochastic as they are computed based on random samples. As described by Kleywegt *et al.*, the values for $\hat{x}$ and $V$ get closer to the optimal values and the objective value of the original problem, with a probability of approximately one, as the sample size increases [13]. Thus, with a moderately large sample size, SAA scheme provides relatively good solutions to the original problem.

Key steps of the SAA algorithm are as follows:

1. Set iteration count to zero; $SAA_{LB}$ to zero; $SAA_{UB}$ to $\infty$; and, the optimality gap to $\alpha$. Generate $M$ independent samples of size $|\Omega|$ and solve the SAA problem (Eq. 4) for each sample. For sample $n$, let $\hat{x}^n$ and $V^n$ represent the optimal solution and the optimal objective value respectively.
2. Compute the average of the optimal objective values over all samples, $\bar{V}$, which provides a statistical lower bound of the optimal objective value of the original problem. The average $\bar{V}$ and its associated variance $\sigma_{\bar{V}}^2$ are computed as follows:

$$\bar{V} := \tfrac{1}{M} \sum_{n=1}^{M} (V^n)$$

$$\sigma_{\bar{V}}^2 := \tfrac{1}{(M-1)M} \sum_{n=1}^{M} (V^n - \bar{V})^2$$

Update variable $SAA_{LB} = \bar{V}$.
3. Select a feasible solution $\bar{x}$ of the true problem from the solutions computed in Step 1. Generate an independent reference sample of size $|\Omega_R|$, much larger than the sample size used in computing the solutions $\hat{x}^n$. Using this reference sample and one of the feasible solutions, estimate the objective function value of the true problem as follows:

$$\hat{f}(\bar{x}) := \sum_{t=1}^{T} \sum_{j=1}^{N} S_j \bar{x}_{jt} + \tfrac{1}{|\Omega_R|} \sum_{s=1}^{|\Omega_R|} Q(\bar{x}, \omega^s)$$

Update the variable $SAA_{UB} = \hat{f}(\bar{x})$. Usually, $\bar{x}$ chosen from $\hat{x}^n$ results in the smallest value for $\hat{f}(\bar{x})$. Variance of the estimate, $\hat{f}(\bar{x})$, can be computed using Eq. 5.
4. If $(SAA_{UB} - SAA_{LB}) \leq \alpha$ then go to next step. Else, go to Step 1.
5. Compute an estimate of the optimality gap and the associated variance as follows:

$$Gap := SAA_{UB} - SAA_{LB}$$

$$\sigma_{gap}^2 = \sigma^2(\bar{x}) + \sigma_{\bar{V}}^2.$$

$$\sigma^2(\bar{x}) := \frac{1}{(|\Omega_R|-1)\,|\Omega_R|} + \sum_{s=1}^{|\Omega_R|} \left( \sum_{t=1}^{T} \sum_{j=1}^{N} S_j \bar{x}_{jt} + Q(\bar{x},\omega^s) - \hat{f}(\bar{x}) \right) \quad (5)$$

$$LB = min \sum_{t=1}^{T}\sum_{j=1}^{N} S_j x_{jt} + \theta \quad (6a)$$

$$s.t. \quad \sum_{t'=t}^{min\{T, t+(u1-1)\}} x_{jt'} \leq 1 \qquad \forall j \in J_{NS1}, \forall t \in T \quad (6b)$$

$$\sum_{t'=t}^{min\{T, t+(u2-1)\}} x_{jt'} \leq 1 \qquad \forall j \in J_{NS2}, \forall t = 1,..,T \quad (6c)$$

$$\theta \geq \sum_{t=1}^{T} a_t^k + \sum_{t=1}^{T} \sum_{j \in J_{OND}} b_{jt}^k x_{jt} \quad (6d)$$

$$+ \sum_{t=1}^{T} \sum_{j \in J_{NS1}} c_{jt}^{k} \left( \sum_{t=max\{1,t-(u1-1)\}}^{t} x_{jt} \right) \tag{6e}$$

$$+ \sum_{t=1}^{T} \sum_{j \in J_{NS2}} d_{jt}^{k} \left( \sum_{t=max\{1,t-(u2-1)\}}^{t} x_{jt} \right) \tag{6f}$$

$$Q(\hat{x}^{k}, \omega) = min \sum_{t=1}^{T} \sum_{j=1}^{N} C_j P_{jt}^{\omega} + \sum_{t=1}^{T} \lambda l_t^{\omega} \tag{7a}$$

$$s.t. \quad \sum_{j=1}^{N} P_j(P_{jt}^{\omega}) + l_t^{\omega} \geq d_t^{\omega} \qquad \forall t = 1,..,T \quad (\pi) \tag{7b}$$

$$P_{jt}^{\omega} \leq \hat{x}_{jt}^{k} \qquad \forall j \in J_{OND}, \forall t = 1,...,T \quad (\mu) \tag{7c}$$

$$P_{jt}^{\omega} \leq \sum_{t'=max\{1,t-(u1-1)\}}^{t} \hat{x}_{jt'}^{k} \qquad \forall j \in J_{NS1}, \forall t = 1,..,T \quad (\gamma) \tag{7d}$$

$$P_{jt}^{\omega} \leq \sum_{t'=max\{1,t-(u2-1)\}}^{t} \hat{x}_{jt'}^{k} \qquad \forall j \in J_{NS2}, \forall t = 1,..,T \quad (\rho) \tag{7e}$$

$$0 \leq P_{jt}^{\omega} \leq 1 \qquad \forall j \in J, \forall t = 1,..,T \tag{7f}$$

## 4.2   L-Shaped Decomposition Algorithm

We detail the L-shaped decomposition algorithm that we used in the SAA algorithm. In the SAA algorithm, we solve the sample average problem (Eq. 4) for each sample, which is a two-stage stochastic programming problem with a finite number of scenarios. We use the L-shaped decomposition algorithm to solve the sample average problem for each sample. The algorithm can be described as follows:

1. Let $LB = 0$, $UB = \infty$, iteration counter $k = 0$, and optimality gap be $\epsilon$. Solve the following lower bound formulation (Master problem) to get the lower bound of the algorithm as given by Eq. 6, where $\hat{x}^k$ is the optimal solution of the Master problem at iteration $k$.
2. Given $\hat{x}^k$, solve the second-stage problem for each scenario $\omega$, described by Eq. 7. The dual variables corresponding to the constraints are represented by symbols: $\pi, \mu, \gamma$, and $\rho$.
3. Use the objective values of all the second-stage problems to compute the total objective function value at iteration $k$, as follows:

$$f(\hat{x}^k) = \sum_{t=1}^{T} \sum_{j=1}^{N} S_j \hat{x}_{jt}^k + \frac{1}{|\Omega|} \sum_{\omega \in \Omega} Q(\hat{x}^k, \omega).$$

If $f(\hat{x}^k) < UB$, update the upper bound $UB = f(\hat{x}^k)$, and store the solution $\hat{x} = \hat{x}^k$.
4. If $(UB - LB) < \epsilon$, then stop, and return $\hat{x}$ as the optimal solution and $UB$ as the optimal objective value. Otherwise, go to Step 5.

5. Use optimal dual solutions of each second-stage problems corresponding to scenarios, $\omega = 1, 2, 3, ..., |\Omega|$, from Step 2 to compute the coefficients of optimality constraints. Aggregate the coefficients of the optimality constraints from all the scenarios to compute the coefficients of the aggregated optimality constraint (cut) as follows:

$$a_t^{k+1} = \frac{1}{|\Omega|} \sum_{\omega \in \Omega} \hat{\pi}_t^\omega d_t^\omega$$
$$b_{jt}^{k+1} = \frac{1}{|\Omega|} \sum_{\omega \in \Omega} \hat{\mu}_{jt}^\omega$$
$$c_{jt}^{k+1} = \frac{1}{|\Omega|} \sum_{\omega \in \Omega} \hat{\gamma}_{jt}^\omega$$
$$d_{jt}^{k+1} = \frac{1}{|\Omega|} \sum_{\omega \in \Omega} \hat{\rho}_{jt}^\omega.$$

Now, construct the new optimality cut with these coefficients and add the cut to the Master problem. Update $k = k + 1$ and go to Step 1.

We empirically evaluated the efficacy of the integrated SAA and L-shaped decomposition approach using two synthetic datasets that were inspired from the Belle II experiment and real-world data from cloud computing platforms. We provide the details in Sect. 6. We describe the genetic algorithms based approach next.

## 4.3    A Genetic Algorithms Based Approach

Genetic Algorithms (GA) are common evolutionary optimization techniques that are used to solve problems containing large and complex search spaces. GAs emulate the process of natural selection to produce better solutions as time progresses. GAs consist of a set of candidate solutions called a population. Each solution within the population is called a chromosome. Chromosomes can be compared with one another by evaluating their fitness, i.e., how well they optimize a given objective. Individual decision variables within a chromosome are called genes. During the execution of a GA, various genetic operations (e.g., mutation of individual genes, swapping genes between chromosomes) are performed to enable progress through the search space.

A GA based approach for cost-efficient selection and scheduling of resources with demand uncertainty was introduced in [6]. This method implements a multi-objective Genetic algorithm based on NSGA-II [5]. In this approach, genes represent individual months within the planning horizon, and will specify the amount of each resource type allocated for that month. Chromosome are represented as $P \times Q$ matrices, where $P$ and $Q$ represent the number of months and the number of resource types available, respectively. If the resources determined by a chromosome are unable to meet the specified demand, additional on-demand resources are subscribed to fill the gap. To speed up evaluation of the search space, parallel execution of the GA is achieved using a modified island model. We refer you to Friese et al., for further details [6]. The primary reason to consider this algorithm in the paper is to provide a baseline evaluation of the two-stage stochastic programming approach.

# 5 Experimental Setup

Computation and data storage of Belle II experiments span a geographically distributed set of resources across several continents. The experiments can be classified into three main activities: (i) processing of raw data from the Belle II detector, (ii) Monte Carlo simulations of physical phenomena, and (iii) physics analysis of experimental and simulation data. While the computational demand for Monte Carlo campaigns is fairly stable, the demand for user analysis tends to be chaotic leading to uncertainties in computational and storage demands. Inspired from this setting, we use a representative setup for demand and supply in our experiments that are detailed in this section.

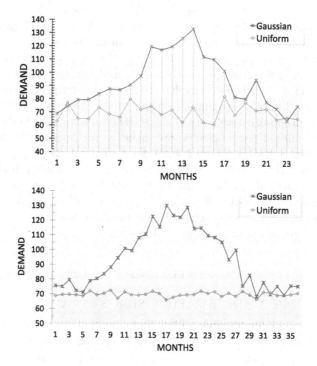

**Fig. 1.** Base demand curves for 24 months (top) and 36 months (bottom) with uniform and Gaussian distributions.

Numerical experiments are conducted for 24-month and 36-month planning horizons. Additionally, for each planning horizon, we study two probability distributions – uniform and Gaussian. For each distribution, we construct five unique base demand curves. Figure 1 illustrates base demand curves for uniform and Gaussian distributions over a 24-month (left) and 36-month (right) planning horizons. Each base demand curve is used to construct random demand scenarios. Specifically, for each month in the base curve, a uniform distribution,

$U(d_b - a, d_b + b)$, is sampled to realize the actual demand for the corresponding month in a given scenario. We conduct experiments to evaluate scenarios that were constructed using two different levels of variation: smaller variation, $U(d_b - 7.5, d_b + 15)$, and larger variation, $U(d_b - 15, d_b + 20)$. All experiments are carried out for 10 SAA samples, where each sample consists of 80 scenarios. The size of the reference sample is set to 1000 scenarios. Our experimental results will show that these parameters of SAA can obtain good quality solutions and can provide better approximation of the true problem.

We use representative computation and cost models of cloud computing resources based on Amazon EC2, as shown in Table 2. ECU, Period, $S$, and $C$ respectively denote computing power, subscription period, subscription cost (in dollars), and usage cost per month for each machine. We only list a subset of machine types for illustrative purposes. A full list is provided in [6]. Please note that the prices in the table may not reflect current Amazon EC2 prices. In our experiments, we assume that we can purchase/utilize no more than 10 units of a resource for any given month. We implement the integrated Sample Average Approximation and the L-shaped decomposition algorithm in Python 2.7 with Gurobi optimizer [7] that is used to solve the mixed-integer programming master problem and the linear programming second-stage problems. The experiments are run on a laptop with Intel core i7 2.80 GHz processor and 8 GB RAM. We compare the results of our stochastic optimization methodology with a genetic algorithms based approach (Sect. 4.3). A fundamental difference between the two approaches is that the GA based approach is deterministic, in that it does not consider demand uncertainty during the fitness evaluation of the chromosomes [6]. However, the GA independently evaluates all the demand scenarios as part of the SAA framework. The solution that minimizes cost across all the scenarios is chosen as the best resource allocation strategy.

**Table 2.** A subset of Amazon EC2 resources used in our experiments

| Index | Machine type | ECU | Period | S | C |
|---|---|---|---|---|---|
| 1 | On-demand | 0.2 | 1 | 0 | 19.04 |
| 3 | Hybrid | 0.2 | 12 | 102 | 4.38 |
| 4 | Subscription | 0.2 | 12 | 151 | 0 |
| 18 | On-demand | 13 | 12 | 0 | 126.29 |
| 19 | Hybrid | 13 | 12 | 648 | 54.02 |
| 20 | Subscription | 13 | 12 | 1271 | 0 |
| 33 | On-demand | 124.5 | 12 | 0 | 1264.36 |
| 34 | Hybrid | 124.5 | 12 | 6482 | 540.2 |
| 35 | Subscription | 124.5 | 12 | 12706 | 0 |

# 6    Experimental Results

We now present the results and observations from our experiments. We will first analyze the solutions computed by the two-stage stochastic programming approach by studying the convergence, variation and composition of the solutions. We will then assess the quality of solutions relative to deterministic solutions that do not include demand uncertainty. We will finally look at the quality with respect to the solutions computed by the Genetic Algorithms based approach.

## 6.1    Stochastic Programming Based Solutions

**Convergence:** Each sample in the Sample Average Approximation (SAA) problem is solved using the L-shaped decomposition algorithm. Performance of L-shaped algorithm is therefore critical for the overall performance. We analyze the convergence behavior of the L-shaped algorithm. Figure 2 illustrates convergence of the upper and lower bounds of the algorithm over iterations for a sample with 24-month horizon. As the samples are randomly generated, the optimal cost at which the algorithm converges for different samples vary within a small range which is evident from Table 3 where the variances associated with the optimal costs are In general, we observe that the upper bound of the algorithm decreases over iterations as the Master problem produces better solutions at each iteration until convergence. Similarly, the lower bound increases as the optimality constraints force the Master problem to purchase the best possible machines to satisfy demands. The algorithm converges when no better machine configurations are available to reduce the total cost. At which point, the upper and lower bounds of the algorithm converge to the same value.

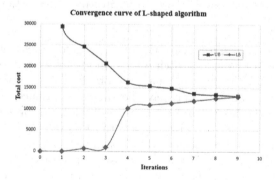

**Fig. 2.** Convergence of the L-shaped algorithm fora sample with 24-month horizon.

**Composition:** With explicit consideration of demand uncertainties, the proposed solutions compute optimal machine subscriptions that are robust against random demand scenarios. The solutions also indicate the optimal subscription time for each selected resource since we assume that the resources can be used partially for a given period. Thus, the composition of the solution – different machines selected in the optimal solution – is an important factor. Intuitively, a cost-effective decision is to subscribe total-upfront or partial-upfront (hybrid) machines at the beginning of the planning horizon and then use them to the maximum extent at each time period to meet the demand. Smaller portions of unmet demand can be satisfied by on-demand machines. In Fig. 3, we illustrate the machine composition for a 24-month planning horizon where the base demands follow a Gaussian distribution. We observe that a large portion of the demand is satisfied by partial-upfront (hybrid) resources, and the rest of the demands are satisfied by on-demand resources.

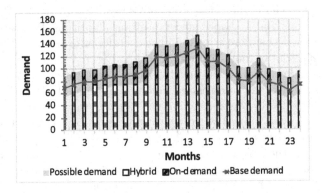

**Fig. 3.** Composition of the solution for a problem with 24-month horizon. The orange shaded region shows possible variation of demand from the base curve shown in red. Each bar represents machine type composition for a given month. Hybrid (partial upfront) machines shown in blue are purchased during Period 1, and used in subsequent periods. On-demand purchases are shown with hatched blue bars. (Color figure online)

**Variance:** Since SAA approximates the true problem by a set of scenarios, the total cost computed by our approach is only an approximation of the true cost (Sect. 4.1). Therefore, we now present data on the variance of the estimates, $\sigma^2_{gap}$, from their true values. Intuitively, the lower the variance, the better is the approximation of the SAA-based solution. In Table 3, we present the optimal cost and the associated variance for a case with 24-month planning horizon. The base demands follow both Uniform and Gaussian distributions, and with smaller and larger variation (Sect. 5). The optimal cost is the total cost corresponding to the optimal solution, where the total cost consists of the total subscription cost and the expected operating cost over all the scenarios. We observe that the variance is small, which indicates that our approach provides high quality estimates of the true problem. We also observe that the variance increases as the uncertainty increases. For example, variance is larger for larger variation runs, and for Gaussian distributions. Consequently, the solutions include subscription of machines with larger computing power to satisfy penalties from large variations in demand, which in turn, increases the total cost.

**Table 3.** Variance of the approximate solutions for a 24-month case

| Smaller variation | | Larger variation | |
|---|---|---|---|
| Uniform distribution | | | |
| Optimal cost | Variance | Optimal cost | Variance |
| 12337.20 | 32.04 | 12640.97 | 150.24 |
| 12216.32 | 29.30 | 12587.71 | 143.50 |
| 12398.36 | 24.45 | 12836.32 | 159.98 |
| 12343.92 | 23.45 | 12786.89 | 153.57 |
| 12543.82 | 27.01 | 13055.08 | 113.92 |
| Gaussian distribution | | | |
| 16942.72 | 23.88 | 17222.81 | 111.41 |
| 16635.05 | 35.41 | 17056.74 | 146.53 |
| 15968.80 | 33.07 | 16265.13 | 155.53 |
| 16612.91 | 30.42 | 17046.62 | 135.45 |
| 17111.34 | 27.85 | 17367.92 | 108.90 |

## 6.2    Value of Stochastic Solution

An important research question of our work is: *How much benefit do we really get from considering demand uncertainty?* To quantify the answer, we use a metric known as *the value of stochastic solution* (VSS). VSS measures the difference between the optimal cost resulting from a solution considering uncertainty and the optimal cost resulting from applying the expected value problem (EVP) to uncertain scenarios. Mathematically, $VSS = \frac{EVC-SPC}{SPC}$. Here, $EVC$ represents the total cost from applying the solution of $EVP$ on the random scenarios, whereas $SPC$ represents the total cost resulting from the stochastic programming solution. EVP is a deterministic problem where the expected value of the random demands over all the scenarios are used. If the solution of the EVP is applied to an uncertain environment, it is likely that the resulting cost will be larger than the cost from applying a stochastic programming solution. Due to explicit consideration of uncertainty, the stochastic programming based solution is robust to uncertain demands. The larger the value of VSS, the larger is the cost of ignoring uncertainty for a problem that is actually uncertain.

In Table 4, we present VSS values for five different problems with a 24-month horizon with base demand curves generated from a Gaussian distribution. We observe that the total cost from using the deterministic solution in an uncertain environment is larger than the cost resulting from a stochastic programming solution. We also observe that VSS increases as the range of uncertainty in demand increases. With large uncertainties, EVP gets erroneous and leads to purchase decisions with larger number of underutilized machines, or reliance on on-demand (spot pricing) with higher penalty costs. The VSS values obtained for the problem instances with based demand curves generated from a Uniform distribution also demonstrates the similar behavior as discussed above.

**Table 4.** Value of stochastic solution for 24-months with Gaussian demand curves

| Smaller variation | | | Larger variation | | |
|---|---|---|---|---|---|
| SPC | EVC | VSS (%) | SPC | EVC | VSS (%) |
| 16942.72 | 19992.45 | 18.02 | 17222.81 | 22326.62 | **29.63** |
| 16635.05 | 19562.82 | 17.60 | 17056.74 | 22148.01 | **29.85** |
| 15968.80 | 18518.86 | 15.97 | 16265.13 | 20196.25 | 24.17 |
| 16612.91 | 19486.94 | 17.29 | 17046.62 | 22013.15 | **29.14** |
| 17111.34 | 19986.04 | 16.80 | 17367.92 | 22170.15 | 27.65 |

## 6.3   Comparison with a GA-Based Approach

As the last part of our evaluation, we compare the quality of our approach with respect to a genetic algorithm (GA) based approach of Friese *et al.* [6] We summarize the results in Table 5 for a problem with 36-month planning horizon and base demand curves with Gaussian distribution. We observe that the stochastic programming based approach significantly outperforms the GA based approach by up to **54%**. Since GA is a heuristic, there are no guarantees for the quality of solutions. Further, the GA-based approach addresses uncertainties indirectly from solving all the scenarios independently and picking the best solution. In contrast, our approach improves the Master solution by systematically considering each scenario. We also observe that the total cost of the solution computed

**Table 5.** Comparison with the GA based approach for 36-months with Gaussian demand curves The cost reduction (%) is the percentage reduction in the total cost provided by the solution from SAA integrated L-shaped approach compared to the GA based approach

| Smaller variation | | |
|---|---|---|
| Total cost (SAA+L-sh) | Total cost (GA) | Cost reduction (%) |
| 20390.94 | 31773.69 | 35.82 |
| 19947.72 | 34206.53 | **41.68** |
| 20529.12 | 30624.64 | 32.97 |
| 20225.67 | 27842.28 | 27.36 |
| 20120.93 | 34748.06 | **42.09** |
| Larger variation | | |
| Total cost (SAA+L-sh) | Total cost (GA) | Cost reduction (%) |
| 20834.15 | 34157.65 | 39.00 |
| 20624.69 | 35600.94 | 42.07 |
| 20835.65 | 41864.19 | **50.23** |
| 20546.52 | 44433.39 | **53.76** |
| 20443.74 | 33946.73 | 39.78 |

by GA gets larger with larger variation in the data. We are currently exploring methods to improve the overall quality of the GA-based approach.

# 7  Related Work

Our work is motivated by a general lack of rigorous optimization approaches for workflow scheduling with uncertainties. Towards this end, we introduced demand uncertainty in computing the cost-efficient resource allocation of distributed resources for execution of high energy physics workflows. Our work is closely related to resource allocation problem in cloud computing. Much of the existing literature in cloud computing ignores uncertainty in resource allocation problems [10,22]. While a few studies consider uncertainty in demand for cloud computing resources, the uncertainties modeled are from a service provider's perspective. For example, fuzzy optimization is used by Johannes *et al.*, for resource allocation with uncertainty in demand to provide better service to consumers [12]. Similarly, Kusic *et al.*, consider uncertainty in workloads in an optimization framework to provide resources to customers [14]. Resource allocation problems in cloud computing are also explored by several other researchers [16,17,23].

In this paper, we build on our previous work, where we introduced a cost-efficient resource selection framework with demand uncertainties using Sample Average Approximation and Genetic Algorithms [6]. We provide a detailed comparison with this approach in Sect. 6. Our work is also inspired from the Unit Commitment problem in electric power grids [8]. Stochastic programming is widely used to provide resource allocation decisions under uncertainty in many areas including unit commitment problems [24], power generation and transmission line expansion problem [11], and cyber security [2]. Stochastic programming has also been utilized in cloud computing resource management problems [4], in which VM's are reserved or purchased on demand for a given time period, reservations that span more than a single time-period are not considered. However, stochastic programming has not been widely applied for cost-efficient resource selection problems from a user's perspective, and in the context of scientific workflows. To the best of our knowledge, this is the first work to develop a two-stage stochastic programming model and stochastic optimization algorithm for selection of geographically distributed resources under demand uncertainty for efficient execution of complex scientific workflows.

# 8  Conclusions and Future Work

Efficient utilization of geographically distributed resources in the context of large scientific workflows is a challenging problem. We presented a novel stochastic programming based approach for cost-efficient selection of resources under demand uncertainties. By integrating a sampling strategy, Sample Average Approximation with the L-shaped decomposition algorithm, we developed a solution for continuous distribution of the uncertain parameters for demand, capable of solving problems with a large number of scenarios. Using two case studies and two probability distribution functions, we demonstrated the efficacy of the proposed solution. We also demonstrated superior performance relative to a previously developed method using genetic algorithms.

In order to scale the proposed solution approaches to real-world problems, computational complexity needs to be addressed in a systematic manner. Solving a large number of mixed integer problems can be computationally infeasible. One approach can be to approximate this problem by using Lagrange relaxation, which leads to the solution of a large number of small problems. Another approach is to integrate the ideas from this work to develop efficient heuristics to seed the genetic algorithm (GA) based method. Both these methods are part of our ongoing and future work.

In addition to uncertainties in demand, the focus of this work, there are uncertainties in the availability of resources. Further, network and file system congestion lead to uncertainties in system performance. Therefore, the proposed approaches need to be augmented to include these uncertainties without increasing the computational complexity due to the number of scenarios that need to be considered. Systematic analysis of historical demand and supply data can lead to accurate understanding of probability distribution functions, and in turn benefit SAA-based methods. We are collecting a large amount of historical data from the execution of Belle II jobs towards this end.

To the best of our knowledge, this is the first stochastic programming based approach to address the resource allocation problem with demand uncertainties for large-scale scientific workflows. We believe that our work will inspire the development of scheduling methods with explicit consideration of uncertainties – an important problem in distributed computing.

**Acknowledgements.** This work was supported by the Integrated End-to-end Performance Prediction and Diagnosis for Extreme Scientific Workflows (IPPD) Project. IPPD is funded by the U.S. Department of Energy Awards FWP-66406 and DE-SC0012630 at the Pacific Northwest National Laboratory. The work of Luis de la Torre was supported in part by the U.S. Department of Energy, Office of Science, Office of Workforce Development for Teachers and Scientists (WDTS) under the Visiting Faculty Program (VFP).

# References

1. Benders, J.F.: Partitioning procedures for solving mixed-variables programming problems. Numerische mathematik **4**(1), 238–252 (1962)
2. Bhuiyan, T.H., Nandi, A.K., Medal, H., Halappanavar, M.: Minimizing expected maximum risk from cyber-attacks with probabilistic attack success. In: 2016 IEEE Symposium on Technologies for Homeland Security (HST), pp. 1–6. IEEE (2016)
3. Birge, J.R., Louveaux, F.: Introduction to Stochastic Programming, 2nd edn. Springer Publishing Company, New York (2011). https://doi.org/10.1007/978-1-4614-0237-4
4. Chaisiri, S., Lee, B.S., Niyato, D.: Optimization of resource provisioning cost in cloud computing. IEEE Trans. Serv. Comput. **5**(2), 164–177 (2012)

5. Deb, K., Pratap, A., Agarwal, S., Meyarivan, T.: A fast and elitist multiobjective genetic algorithm: Nsga-ii. IEEE Trans. Evol. Comput. **6**(2), 182–197 (2002)
6. Friese, R.D., Halappanavar, M., Sathanur, A.V., Schram, M., Kerbyson, D.J., de la Torre, L.: Towards efficient resource allocation for distributed workflows under demand uncertainties. In: Klusáček, D., Cirne, W., Desai, N. (eds.) JSSPP 2017. LNCS, vol. 10773, pp. 103–121. Springer, Cham (2018). https://doi.org/10.1007/978-3-319-77398-8_6
7. Gurobi, O.: Gurobi optimizer reference manual (2015). http://www.gurobi.com
8. Halappanavar, M., Schram, M., de la Torre, L., Barker, K., Tallent, N.R., Kerbyson, D.J.: Towards efficient scheduling of data intensive high energy physics workflows. In: Proceedings of the 10th Workshop on Workflows in Support of Large-Scale Science, WORKS 2015, pp. 3:1–3:9. ACM, New York, USA (2015)
9. Hara, T.: Belle II: Computing and network requirements. In: Proceedings of the Asia-Pacific Advanced Network, pp. 115–122 (2014)
10. Huang, Z.C., He, C., Gu, L., Wu, J.F.: On-demand service in grid: architecture, design and implementation. In: 2005 Proceedings of 11th International Conference on Parallel and Distributed Systems, vol. 2, pp. 674–678. IEEE (2005)
11. Jirutitijaroen, P., Singh, C.: Reliability constrained multi-area adequacy planning using stochastic programming with sample-average approximations. IEEE Trans. Power Syst. **23**(2), 504–513 (2008)
12. Johannes, A., Borhan, N., Liu, C., Ranjan, R., Chen, J.: A user demand uncertainty based approach for cloud resource management. In: 2013 IEEE 16th International Conference on Computational Science and Engineering (CSE), pp. 566–571. IEEE (2013)
13. Kleywegt, A.J., Shapiro, A., Homem-de Mello, T.: The sample average approximation method for stochastic discrete optimization. SIAM J. Optim. **12**(2), 479–502 (2002)
14. Kusic, D., Kandasamy, N.: Risk-aware limited lookahead control for dynamic resource provisioning in enterprise computing systems. Cluster Comput. **10**(4), 395–408 (2007)
15. Mak, W.K., Morton, D.P., Wood, R.K.: Monte carlo bounding techniques for determining solution quality in stochastic programs. Oper. Res. Lett. **24**(1), 47–56 (1999)
16. Medernach, E., Sanlaville, E.: Fair resource allocation for different scenarios of demands. Eur. J. Oper. Res. **218**(2), 339–350 (2012)
17. Rodriguez, M.A., Buyya, R.: Deadline based resource provisioningand scheduling algorithm for scientific workflows on clouds. IEEE Trans. Cloud Comput. **2**(2), 222–235 (2014)
18. Santoso, T., Ahmed, S., Goetschalckx, M., Shapiro, A.: A stochastic programming approach for supply chain network design under uncertainty. Eur. J. Oper. Res. **167**(1), 96–115 (2005)
19. Saravanan, B., Das, S., Sikri, S., Kothari, D.: A solution to the unit commitment problem-a review. Front. Energy **7**(2), 223 (2013)
20. Shapiro, A., Homem-de Mello, T.: A simulation-based approach to two-stage stochastic programming with recourse. Math. Program. **81**(3), 301–325 (1998)
21. Van Slyke, R.M., Wets, R.: L-shaped linear programs with applications to optimal control and stochastic programming. SIAM J. Appl. Math. **17**(4), 638–663 (1969)
22. Yang, J., Qiu, J., Li, Y.: A profile-based approach to just-in-time scalability for cloud applications. In: 2009 IEEE International Conference on Cloud Computing, CLOUD 2009, pp. 9–16. IEEE (2009)

23. Zhang, Q., Zhu, Q., Boutaba, R.: Dynamic resource allocation for spot markets in cloud computing environments. In: 2011 Fourth IEEE International Conference on Utility and Cloud Computing (UCC), pp. 178–185. IEEE (2011)
24. Zheng, Q.P., Wang, J., Pardalos, P.M., Guan, Y.: A decomposition approach to the two-stage stochastic unit commitment problem. Annal. Oper. Res. **210**(1), 387–410 (2013)

# Approaching Actor-Level Resource Control for Akka

Ahmed Abdelmoamen[1(✉)], Dezhong Wang[2], and Nadeem Jamali[2]

[1] Department of Computer Science, Prairie View A&M University,
Prairie View, TX, USA
amahmed@pvamu.edu
[2] Department of Computer Science, University of Saskatchewan,
Saskatoon, SK, Canada
dew320@mail.usask.ca, jamali@cs.usask.ca

**Abstract.** Although there are models and prototype implementations for controlling resource use in Actor systems, they are difficult to implement for production implementations of Actors such as Akka. This is because the messaging and scheduling infrastructures of runtime systems are increasingly complex and significantly different from one system to another. This paper presents our efforts in implementing resource control support for Actor systems implemented using the Akka library. Particularly, given the lack of support in Akka for direct scheduling of actors, we compare two different ways of approximating actor-level control support. The first implementation expects messages to actors to provide estimates of resources likely to be consumed for processing them; these estimates are then relied upon to make scheduling decisions. In the second implementation, resource use of scheduled actors is tracked, and compared against allocations to decide when they should be scheduled next. We present experimental results on the performance cost of these resource control mechanisms, as well as their impact on resource utilization.

**Keywords:** Resource control · Scala · Akka · Actors

## 1   Introduction

It is becoming increasingly important to control resources in parallel and distributed systems. Consider, for example, a multi-tenant system where the same instance of the system can host services for multiple clients simultaneously. This requires the ability to separate the tenants in the resource space. There is growing demand for cloud services to control and deliver resources at a fine grain.

One way to support the functional needs of such systems is by implementing them using Actors [1]. Actors are autonomous concurrently executing active objects. Actors communicate using asynchronous messages. The model mandates globally unique names for actors, and these names cannot be guessed, making it possible for multiple instances of a service (e.g., tenants) to coexist in the

D. Klusáček et al. (Eds.): JSSPP 2018, LNCS 11332, pp. 127–146, 2019.
https://doi.org/10.1007/978-3-030-10632-4_7

same namespace without interfering with each other. However, managing the resource competition between actors requires additional support for resource coordination, as provided by the CyberOrgs model [2].

There is a growing number of implementations of Actors, including production languages such as Scala [3] which supports actors through its Akka library [4]. Although resource control has been implemented for efficient prototype implementations of Actors [5], none of the production languages currently support it. The specific mechanisms making up these solutions do not easily transfer between languages because of significant differences in their message-handling and scheduling infrastructures. In other words, the opportunities afforded for the required fine-grained scheduling are very specific to each language.

This paper presents our implementation of such support as an extension[1] for Scala/Akka. Particularly, we compare two different ways of supporting resource control for Actor systems in Akka. The first implementation relies on programmer-provided estimates of resources required to process messages; these estimates are then relied upon to make scheduling decisions. The estimates could be obtained analytically or experimentally, manually or automatically. In the second implementation, the system tracks the resource use by actors to process messages; these measurements are then compared against allocations to decide when they should be scheduled next.

The rest of the paper is organized as follows: Sect. 2 presents related work. Section 3 presents the designs and prototype implementations of the two resource control approach we have developed for Akka. Section 4 experimentally establishes the performance cost of using these approaches, as well as their impact on resource utilization. Finally, Sect. 5 concludes the paper.

## 2    Related Work

There has been growing interest in resource control from various perspectives.

One model for coordinating resources in Actor systems is CyberOrgs [6], which creates resource encapsulations called cyberorgs in which actors can execute as long as there are resources. Resources can be traded between cyberorgs. New cyberorgs can be spawned and existing cyberorgs can assimilate into others.

Where early implementations of CyberOrgs controlled resources for actors by controlling how long their threads are scheduled for, more efficient production languages implementing Actors do not dedicate threads to actors. [5] develops a way of controlling resources for actor systems by manipulating the order in which actor messages are delivered for processing.

Selectors [7] extend the Actor model to simplify writing of synchronization and coordination patterns by controlling the order in which messages are processed. Selectors have multiple mailboxes, which allow specifying which mailboxes can deliver the next message, and which must buffer it.

---

[1] Available online: https://github.com/ama883/ActorGroup-Akka-Resource-Control-Lib.

The programming of resource-efficient concurrent applications is discussed in [8] where a C++ Actor framework, CAF, is introduced which aims to provide a scalable environment for building resource-efficient applications and distributed systems based on the Actor Model. CAF provides a way for programmers to monitor the performance of their distributed systems on the runtime through interactive shells, which gives insights about the runtime characteristics of them. CAF also grants programmers a convenient access to aggregated information about resource usage on each node where distributed systems are deployed.

Resource control is also an essential requirement in multi-tenancy where the same instance of the service can serve the needs of multiple clients simultaneously. A requirement for such a system is the ability to manage the resource competition between the tenants. Amusa [9] is a middleware for efficient access control management of multi-tenant Software-as-a-service (SaaS) applications. Amusa enables the service provider to easily constrain the tenants in terms of the hosting server's resources. It allows both the service provider and its tenants' users to express their access rules on the SaaS application level, combines these rules securely and enforces them at run-time.

In multimedia, MASTER [10] provides a set of toolkits to support cross-platform application streaming that is able to utilize elastic resources in the cloud. Application providers can use MASTER to stream their resource-intensive applications from public clouds to remote users using various types of devices. Particularly, providers can deploy their applications in a server located in the cloud, which can be operated to provide multiple streaming sessions simultaneously. This can significantly improve resource utilization of the server. MASTER also provides control over resource acquisition and requests dispatching by leveraging request the arrival patterns and the streaming session lengths.

In cloud computing, Apollo [11] is a task scheduling framework, which has been deployed to schedule jobs in cloud-scale production clusters at Microsoft. Apollo considers future resource availability on all the servers when taking each scheduling decision. Resource monitoring in Apollo is done using a Resource Monitor (RM) component in each cluster. RM aggregates load information from across the cluster continuously and provides a global view of the cluster status to make informed scheduling decisions.

Some commercial solutions have also been proposed for resource use monitoring of concurrent systems such as Kamon [12] and Sematext [13] which provide custom made methods of monitoring resources used by groups of actors. However, these solutions do not provide a way to control resource use. Google also launched the Namespaces API [14] in the Google app engine to support multitenancy in both Java and Python. Using the Namespaces API, data can be easily partitioned across tenants simply by specifying a unique namespace string for each tenant.

## 3   Design and Implementation

To support resource control in an actor system, we need to control the amount of resource used by each actor computation in the system. The most direct way to do so is by controlling the scheduling of the actors' threads [6]. However, efficient production languages such as Scala/Akka do not use one thread per actor; it is orders of magnitude more efficient to have a pool of threads, where each thread executes multiple actors [15]. One possibility could be to have a related group of actors be executed by a thread, and then schedule the threads as required. The performance would then depend on the number of these groups hosted in the system.

A different approach to controlling resources for actors is by manipulating the order in which actor messages are delivered for processing [5]. Although the level of control afforded by this approach is not as precise as what could be possible in a one-thread-per-actor implementation, it offers sufficient control for important classes of applications [5]. In this paper, we apply a similar approach to actor systems implemented in Akka. The main challenge we faced was the very different messaging and scheduling infrastructure in Akka's runtime system, requiring new algorithms to be developed.

We create resource encapsulations for related groups of actors, called *actorgroups*. Each of the actors encapsulated in an actorgroup is called as a *managed actor*. A managed actor must be registered in an actorgroup in order to consume its allocated resources. We manage the resource usage of an actorgroup by controlling the flow of messages sent to its managed actors.

The resource we control in this work is CPU time, counted in 1-millisecond *ticks*. Ticks are consumed by managed actors to execute computations triggered by the arrival of messages. Allocations are made to actorgroups within recurring *time intervals*. If a tick available to an actorgroup in an interval is not consumed, it expires [2]. Allocations to actorgroups are in the form of (ticks-per-interval, number-of-intervals) pairs, and are intended to be applied immediately. Ticks allocated to (and consequently *owned by*) an actorgroup are shared among its managed actors. An actorgroup is marked as inactive after its assigned ticks are consumed by its managed actors.

We compare two ways of supporting resource control for Actor systems implemented using Akka, one assuming that there is a way for programmers to estimate the amount of computation required for processing each message, and the other without such an assumption. We first describe the system components shared between the two approaches, and then discuss the two approaches separately.

### 3.1  Shared Components

*Message Dispatcher.* In Akka, a message dispatcher is considered the *core engine* for the runtime system because it controls the processor cycles given to actors. The dispatcher has access to the global message queue, actors' mailboxes,[2] and the pool of threads which executes the actors. One of the necessary configuration settings to Akka message dispatcher is `throughput`, which defines the number

---

[2] Mailbox is the dispatching unit in Akka, which contains one or more messages that can be processed in sequence during an interval.

of messages delivered to an actor at one time. For example, if the throughput is set to $m$, and the number of messages queued up in the global message queue for an actor is $n$, if $m < n$, $m$ messages are delivered to the actor in one shot, and the remaining messages wait for the next turn.

*ActorGroup Manager.* The ActorGroup Manager is responsible for book-keeping about ticks consumed by managed actors as a result of delivery of messages. A new actorgroup interested in receiving resources registers itself with the Actor-Group Manager. Once the registration request is received, the ActorGroup Manager instantly adds the actorgroup to its resource scheduling, and the actorgroup begins receiving ticks from the next interval on. Although the current implementation does not have the ability to reserve resources not beginning immediately, a new request can be made at runtime for an actorgroup, overriding previous allocations.

*ActorGroup Runnable.* When a message is sent to an actor, the dispatcher first places it in the global message queue. When it is that actor's turn to be executed, the dispatcher queries the ActorGroup Manager about whether the receiving actor is schedulable, by checking whether its owner actorgroup is still active (i.e., still owns ticks in the current interval). If the receiving actor is schedulable, its mailbox is wrapped into an idle thread from the thread pool to create an *ActorGroup Runnable*. The dispatcher then moves the right number of messages for that actor – as determined by the throughput setting – from the global queue to the actor's mailbox, and finally tells the runnable to execute the actor for those messages.

## 3.2   The Two Implementations

Next, we discuss the differing aspects of the two implementations.

**Pre-estimated Execution Time Implementation.** This implementation relies on programmer-provided estimations of ticks required to process messages. These requirements could be estimated analytically or experimentally. We enable the providing of these estimates by defining a new type of actor message which encapsulates expected execution time for a message along with an Akka actor message.

The number of messages delivered to actors' mailboxes is controlled using mechanisms which work within the constraints of Akka's message dispatcher. In particular, we add two new components to Akka's infrastructure. We add a *gate-keeper* to the message dispatcher (see Fig. 1) to decide whether to deliver or postpone the delivery of messages for an actor according to the number of ticks remaining in its actorgroup's allocation for the current interval. We also add an *observer* to an actor's mailbox to observe the number of ticks consumed by it. Additionally, we add book-keeping to keep track of actorgroups, their hosted actors, and their resource allocations. To allow an actorgroup to maximally utilize its allocated ticks for an interval, we replace Akka's default FIFO actor mailbox queues

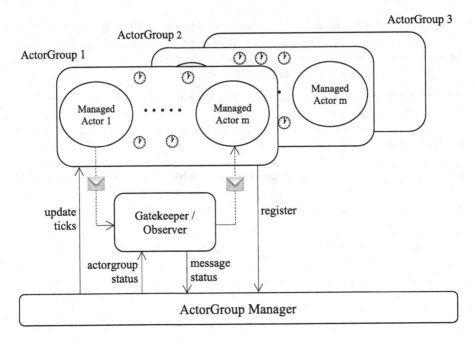

**Fig. 1.** System architecture

with *first-fit* queues. Particularly, in each interval, we begin by delivering messages in FIFO order until a message is encountered which cannot be delivered because not enough allocation remains for the interval; only at that time, the next message which can be delivered within the allocation's constraints is delivered next. This is done as long as time remains in that allocation. Because the too-large message is at the front of the queue for the next interval, and therefore guaranteed execution then, there is no risk of starvation. Although this changes the messages' order of delivery, Actor semantics [1] explicitly allow it.

Figure 2 illustrates how the extension modifies the life cycle of a message. Particularly, note the observer in the actor mailbox and the gatekeeper just below that; the rest of the figure essentially shows Akka's default message dispatching. Once a thread has been given messages for an actor to execute, for each message (beginning with the top message in the first-fit queue), the gatekeeper examines the ticks required for executing it, compares it with the ticks remaining in the actor's actorgroup's allocation for the interval, and executes the actor for the message only if permissible. The observer reports back the actual number of ticks consumed in processing the message, which are then deducted from the actorgroup's allocation for that interval. If the ticks required for the message exceed the actorgroup's remaining allocations for the interval, the thread is returned to the pool, and the actor mailbox (representing the actor's future computations) is placed on a queue of mailboxes waiting for the next interval.

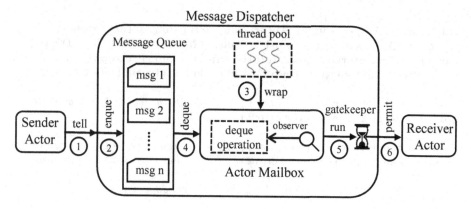

**Fig. 2.** The modified life cycle of message dispatching in the pre-estimated execution time implementation

Figure 3 shows a code snippet illustrating how an actorgroup would be created and allocated processing time in terms of ticks per interval and number of intervals. As mentioned before, our solution is implemented as an extension to Akka where an `ActorGroupExtension` object is used to initialize a new `ActorGroup` object through the `createActorGroup` method. First, a number of configuration variables are set: interval size is set to 1,000 ms; tick size is set to 1 ms which gives us 1,000 ticks per second; the throughput is set to 1.

Two `ActorGroup` objects are initialized: the first actorgroup, `group1`, is assigned 100 ticks per interval for 10 intervals; while the second group, `group2`, is assigned 300 ticks per interval for 10 intervals. In this example, we define two types of managed actors: `lightActor` and `heavyActor`. `lightActor` executes light-weight computations which would take less execution time than the `heavyActor` does. Two instances of `lightActor` and `heavyActor` are registered to `group1` and `group2`, respectively. The `ActorGroupMessage` class is used for creating messages in which the programmer also specifies the number of ticks needed for processing the message. Then ten messages are sent to the four actors in sequence. The system schedules the delivery of these messages according to the allocations of the actorgroups to which the target actors belongs.

**Post-measured Execution Time.** In this implementation, the system measures the actual time taken by managed actors to process messages. To do this, the ActorGroup Runnable adds two hooks, before and after the original message processing respectively, in order to calculate the number of ticks consumed and report the result to the ActorGroup Manager. After a message is processed, the runnable reports the number of ticks consumed in processing it, to the Actor-Group Manager. The ActorGroup Manager then deducts these ticks from the receiving actor's owner actorgroup's allocation for the interval.

One limitation of this implementation is that the ticks required for a message may exceed the actorgroup's remaining allocations for an interval. This leads

```scala
// initialize two ActorGroup instances
var group1 : ActorGroup = ActorGroupExtension ( actorSystem ) .
    createActorGroup ( "group1" , 100 , TimeUnit . MILLISECONDS, 10 )
var group2 : ActorGroup = ActorGroupExtension ( actorSystem ) .
    createActorGroup ( "group2" , 300 , TimeUnit . MILLISECONDS, 20 )

group1 . insertActor ( lightActor1 ) // add lightActor1 to group1
group1 . insertActor ( lightActor2 ) // add lightActor2 to group1

group2 . insertActor ( heavyActor1 ) // add heavyActor1 to group2
group2 . insertActor ( heavyActor2 ) // add heavyActor2 to group2

val r = scala . util .Random // generate random values

/* send 10 messages with different expected execution times to
     both the light and heavy actors */
for { i <- 1 to 10 } {
  lightActor1 ! new ActorGroupMessage ( i , r . nextInt ( 20 ) ,
    TimeUnit . MILLISECONDS )
  lightActor2 ! new ActorGroupMessage ( i , r . nextInt ( 20 ) ,
    TimeUnit . MILLISECONDS )

  heavyActor1 ! new  ActorGroupMessage ( i , r . nextInt ( 50 ) ,
    TimeUnit . MILLISECONDS )
  heavyActor2 ! new  ActorGroupMessage ( i , r . nextInt ( 50 ) ,
    TimeUnit . MILLISECONDS )
}
```

**Fig. 3.** A usage example for the pre-estimated execution time implementation

to a delay in the start times of subsequent intervals. To offset this delay over time, the system does two things. First, it does not schedule the actorgroups exceeding their allocations until after passage of the number of intervals over which those ticks should have been received. Second, it reduces the sizes of subsequent intervals by the number of ticks allocated to the badly behaving (and now unscheduled) actorgroups. A similar approach can also be implemented for the pre-estimated implementation if the programmer provides inaccurate estimations of the ticks required to process messages.

Figure 4 illustrates how the extension modifies the life cycle of a message in the post-measured execution time implementation. Figure 4 is very similar to the one for the pre-estimated execution time Implementation (Fig. 2), except that there is no need for the gatekeeper because this implementation allows messages to be delivered if their receiving actorgroups are still active at the delivery time.

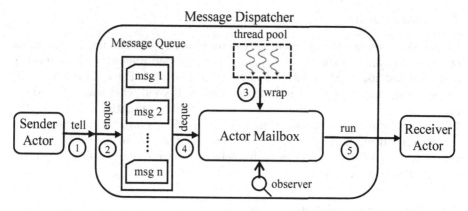

**Fig. 4.** The modified life cycle of message dispatching in the post-measured execution time implementation

A usage example of the post-measured execution time implementation is presented in Fig. 5. This code snippet is very similar to the one for the pre-estimated execution time implementation (Fig. 3), except that there is no need for the `ActorGroupMessage` class because the run-time system measures the actual time taken by managed actors to process messages.

```
// initialize two ActorGroup instances
var group1: ActorGroup = ActorGroupExtension(actorSystem).
    createActorGroup("group1", 100, TimeUnit.MILLISECONDS, 10)
var group2: ActorGroup = ActorGroupExtension(actorSystem).
    createActorGroup("group2", 300, TimeUnit.MILLISECONDS, 20)

group1.insertActor(lightActor1) // add lightActor1 to group1
group1.insertActor(lightActor2) // add lightActor2 to group1

group2.insertActor(heavyActor1) // add heavyActor1 to group2
group2.insertActor(group2) // add heavyActor2 to group2

/* send 10 messages to the light and heavy actors */
for {i <- 1 to 10} {
  lightActor1 ! i
  lightActor2 ! i
  heavyActor1 ! i
  heavyActor2 ! i
}
```

**Fig. 5.** A usage example for the post-measured execution time implementation

# 4   Evaluation

We primarily set out to experimentally determine how our two implementations of a resource control extension compare in terms of performance with each other and with just using Akka without any resource control. For each of these, we measured the time taken per message processed, beyond what was required for processing the message (i.e., carrying out the actual computation). Additionally, for the pre-estimated-execution-time implementation, we measured the system idle time resulting from using the approach. For the post-measured implementation, we studied the impact of badly behaving actor on the quality of control exercised by our extension.

## 4.1   Experimental Setup

Our experiments were carried out on a machine with a 2.6 GHz quad-core Intel i7 processor and 8 GB of RAM, and running Windows 7. We used Scala version 2.11.8 with Akka version 2.4.10 running on JVM 1.8. We set the minimum and the maximum number of active threads in the pool, called parallelism-min and parallelism-max, to 8 and 64, respectively. The parallelism-factor is set to 8. The parallelism-factor is used to determine the thread pool size (i.e., the core number of threads) at start-up, using the formula: `ceil` (available processor's cores x parallelism-factor). The resulting size is then bounded by the parallelism-min and parallelism-max values. However, if a new task is submitted to the pool and there are fewer threads than the maximum pool size, an additional thread will be created as long as the maximum pool size is not exceeded. The parallelism-min, parallelism-max and parallelism-factor settings for each pool of threads provide a way to dynamically size these pools based on the number of CPU cores available.

We generated a set of artificial message loads to simulate the sending of messages to different actors hosted in multiple actorgroups. To simulate real(istic) applications, the time required for processing these messages, and the number of actors per actorgroup is distributed over a normal distribution function. For example, we picked random values with a mean of 10 ms to represent the processing time of a message. We also picked the number of managed actors per actorgroup using the same method.

For all our experiments, we set the interval size to 1,000 ms. To avoid adding the registration delay to our measurements, we started our measurements at the beginning of the first interval after all actorgroups had been registered. For each experiment, the 1,000 ms interval size is evenly divided between the actorgroups used in the experiment. In other words, the time allocation to each actorgroup in an experiment equals to 1,000 ms divided by the number of actorgroups in that experiment.

Each experiment was carried out 10 times.

## 4.2   Overheads

There are three potential sources of significant overhead in our resource control extension. They are related to three types of context switches taking place in the

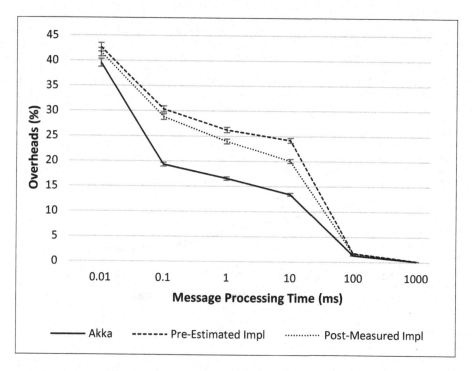

**Fig. 6.** The effect of changing the message time on the per-message overhead percentage: exponential scale

system: message-to-message, actor-to-actor, and thread-to-thread. We carried out a set of experiments to determine the impact of each.

In order to isolate the impact of each parameter on the performance of our two approaches for resource control, wherever possible, we varied one parameter while setting all other parameters to values for which our approaches performed close to Akka (without resource control). These values were determined by trial-and-error.

**Message-to-Message Context Switching.** We ran a set of experiments to determine the impact of message-to-message context switches, which happen when one message's execution completes and the next message's execution begins. We used 100 actorgroups, each hosting 1 actor; 100 messages were sent to each actor. The throughput parameter was set to 100. Figures 6 and 7 show how the message processing time impacted the added overheads for the default Akka, pre-estimated execution time implementation and post-measured execution time implementation. Figure 6 shows that the curves diverge significantly between 10 ms and 100 ms message processing times. Figure 7 shows this on a linear scale between these two points, where the divergence begins to happen around 50 ms, meaning that the added control of our approaches comes at negligible

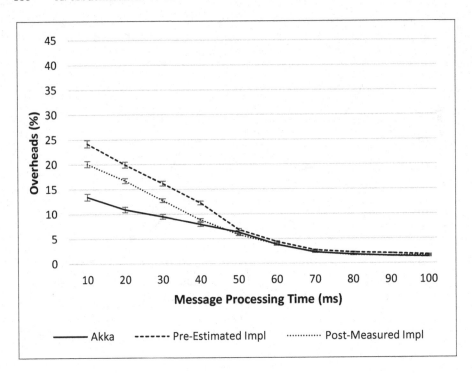

**Fig. 7.** The effect of changing the message time on the per-message overhead percentage: linear scale

cost for coarser-grained tasks, with message execution times above 50 ms. For tasks smaller than that, neither native Akka nor Akka with our extensions has affordable overheads. Also, note that the overheads for the pre-estimated implementation are slightly higher than those for the post-measure one; we believe this to be because of the additional per-message check for whether the actorgroup has sufficient ticks in the current interval to deliver the message to its target actor.

**Actor-to-Actor Context Switching.** There are two potential sources of overhead in actor-to-actor context switches. First, the throughput setting, determining the number of messages an actor can process together at a time. Second, synchronization required for book-keeping about the hosting actorgroup's remaining resources.

We carried out a set of experiments to see the effect of changing the `throughput` parameter on performance. We used 100 actorgroups each containing 1 managed actor; 100 messages were sent to each actor. Each message required 100 ms to be processed.

Figure 8 shows the results. Although the overhead stays roughly between 14% and 15% for Akka without resource control, it ranges from about 17% to 24%

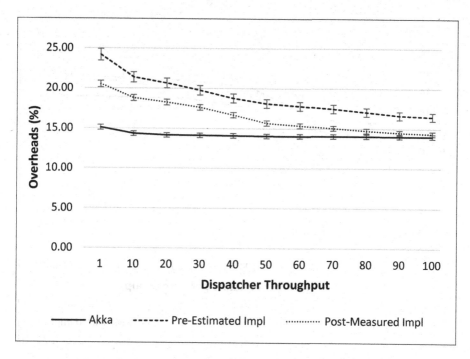

**Fig. 8.** The effect of changing the dispatcher throughput config on the per-message overhead percentage

for the pre-estimated implementation, and from about 14% to 21% for post-measured. This represents an additional 0–3% overhead for the 100 throughput case, and an additional 6–9% additional overhead for the 1 throughput case, where an actor only processes one message at a time. These results suggest that it will be important to have high throughput values – and correspondingly a larger number of available messages for actors to process – to keep this overhead low.

The other potential source of overhead is the synchronized access to the variable `current-number-of-ticks` tracking the number of ticks remaining in the actorgroup's allocation in the current interval. There is a separate variable for each actorgroup. Because this variable needs to be read before allowing a message to be delivered to an actor, and needs to be revised every time one of the concurrently executing actors finishes processing messages, access to the variable needs to be synchronized.

We ran two sets of experiments, one to determine the impact of increasing the number of actors hosted by an actor group, and another to determine the impact of increasing the number of actorgroups while keeping actors-per-actorgroup constant.

For the first set of experiments, we used one actorgroup, and sent 10 messages to each actor hosted by it. A message required 100 ms to be processed. `throughput` was set to 10. Figure 9 shows the effect of changing the number of

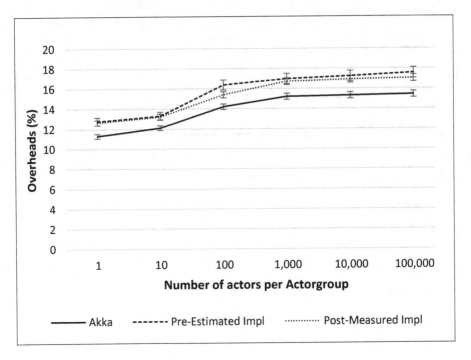

**Fig. 9.** The effect of number of actors per actorgroup on the per-message overhead percentage

actors per actorgroup on the added overheads. There is between about 1.4% and 2.1% additional overhead on top of Akka's own overhead over the wide range between 1 actor per actorgroup and 100,000 actors per actorgroup. It turns out that this overhead is explained by the suboptimal value of 10 we used for the `throughput` – instead of 100; a higher throughput would not have been meaningful because only 10 messages were sent to any actor. We ran an experiment to measure the additional overhead of our solutions on top of Akka's when the `throughput` is set to 100, and the number of messages is set to 100 as well. This additional overhead of our solutions on top of Akka's was found to be between about 1.3% and 1.9%, accounting for a large part of the 1.4% and 2.1% gap observed in Fig. 9. In other words, the number of actors per actorgroup is not a significant contributor to added overhead of our approaches.

For the second set of experiments, each actorgroup hosted 1 actor, and 100 messages were sent to each actor. A message required 100 ms for being processed. `throughput` was set to 100. Figure 10 shows the results. Where the per-message overhead of using Akka without resource control support stays constant around 15% with respect to the number of actorgroups, although it is between 15% and 16% for our two approaches for 1,000 or more actorgroups, it begins rising logarithmically (as suggested by linear increase over exponential scale) to between 23% and 24% for a single actorgroup. This suggests that our approach performs best

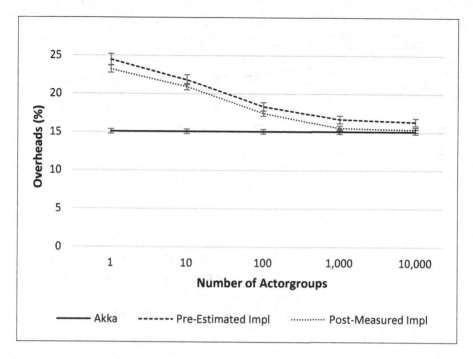

**Fig. 10.** The effect of the number of actorgroups on the per-message overhead percentage

for larger numbers of actorgroups. For fewer actorgroups, resource control comes at a cost which increases logarithmically as the number of actorgroups decreases.

**Thread-to-Thread Context Switching.** The primary factor which affects the thread-to-thread type of context switching is the number of threads active in the system. The JVM scheduler decides the share of CPU cycles given to each active thread in the pool; then the scheduler switches from executing one thread to the next in the thread queue. We carried out a set of experiments to see the effect of changing the number of active threads in the pool on performance.

For this set of experiments, we used 100 actorgroups each of which contains 1 managed actor. 100 messages were sent to each actor, each requiring 100 ms to process. `throughput` was set to 100. In order to precisely control the number of active threads, we set the `parallelism-min` and `parallelism-max` parameters to the same value.

Figure 11 shows the effect of changing the number of active threads on overheads. There appears to be relatively little impact of the number of threads on overhead for all cases for thread pool sizes greater than 8; for lower sizes, there is a logarithmic increase (suggested by linear increase on the exponential scale). There is virtually a constant performance difference between Akka (without resource control) and the post-measured implementation (of about 4%) and

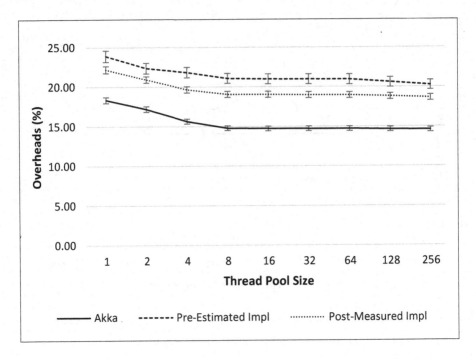

**Fig. 11.** Effect of changing thread pool size on per-message overhead

the pre-estimated implementation (of about 5% to 6%). 2.4% and 3.3%, respectively, of this overhead is accounted for by our use of 100 actorgroups for the experiment (see Fig. 10).

The higher overheads observed for the resource control extensions are because of the (known to be) suboptimal settings we used for throughput, message processing time, and the number of actorgroups.

### 4.3 Idle Time for Pre-estimated Execution Time Implementation

In the pre-estimated execution-time implementation, if the remaining allocation for an actorgroup is insufficient to process any messages in the first-fit queue, the system remains idle until the beginning of the next interval.

We carried out a set of experiments to determine the percentage of idle time per interval as message processing time varies between 10 and 100. We used 10 actorgroups each hosting only 1 actor. 100 messages were sent to each actor. throughput was set to 100, meaning that all messages were always immediately delivered to each actor. As shown in Fig. 12, as the message processing time increases, the chance of having fully-utilized intervals decreases, and accordingly the percentage of idle time per interval increases. Most notably, we found that the percentage of idle time per interval stabilizes at 4.9% beyond 90 ms message processing time. This needs to be viewed in the context that an interval is of 1,000 ms duration, and if each actorgroup has a share of 100 ms on average,

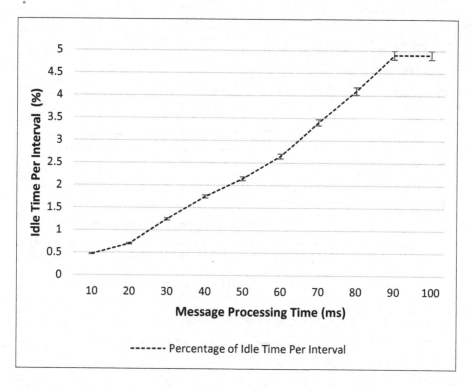

**Fig. 12.** Percentage of idle time per interval in pre-estimated execution-time implementation

roughly half the times, the $10^{th}$ actorgroup will not be served in the interval because serving it would exceed the 1,000 ms limit for the interval. This would lead to an average of 50 ms of idle time, which is 5% of 1,000 ms. This happens because the granularity of allocation (i.e., each actorgroup's share) is 10% of the time interval. In other words, the maximum idle time can be expected to be half of the granularity of allocation.

## 4.4  Quality of Control

We finally examined the level of quality of control achieved by the post-measured execution-time implementation in the face of actorgroups using ticks in excess of their allocations. Recall that we reduce the size of the interval when an actorgroup uses excess resource in an interval. The degree of this downsizing becomes a convenient measure of the impact of badly behaving actorgroups.

We simulated the bad behavior by running a number of badly behaving actorgroups with their over-allocation times distributed over a long-tail Poisson distribution function. Specifically, we used 100 actorgroups, each hosting 1 actor. 1 message is sent to each actor at the beginning of each interval, each requiring an average of 10 ms processing time, so that each actorgroup has a share of 10 ms

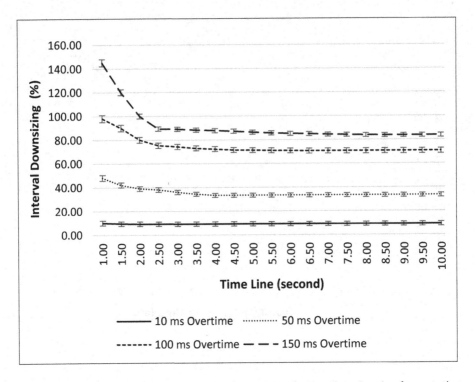

**Fig. 13.** The level of quality of control in the measured-execution-time implementation

per interval, given that the interval size, as always, was set to 1,000 ms. The over-uses we experimented with were averaged at 10 ms, 50 ms, 100 ms and 150 ms overtime per message. We restrict that over-uses to only 10% of the number of actorgroups in our experiment. This is translated to a cumulative of 100 ms, 500 ms, 1,000 ms and 1,500 ms overtime per interval. `throughput` was set to 10. Then we measured the percentage of interval downsizing to assess the impact of this bad behavior.

Figure 13 shows the results. The percentage of interval downsizing decreases over time, and eventually stabilized for all four cases. This means that our extension can bound the effect of that continuous bad behavior over time.

## 5    Conclusions and Future Work

In this paper, we presented an approach to support resource control for Actor systems in Akka. Particularly, we described our design and implementation of two different Akka extensions which work within the constraints of Akka's messaging and scheduling infrastructure, to control resources for groups of actors.

We carried out several sets of experiments in order to establish sources of overheads, paying particular attention to three types of context switches happening in the system. The results showed that the overhead depends on various granularity characteristics of the systems, most notably the sizes of the computations resulting from individual messages, the opportunity to process a large number of messages at a time, and the sizes of the actor groups being provided resources.

In additional sets of experiments, we looked at the impact of message processing times in the pre-estimated execution-time approach on resource utilization of the system. The resulting idle time was found to be related to the granularity of resource allocation. We also looked at the impact of badly behaving actor (i.e., actors using excessive resource) in the post-measured implementation on the quality of control exercised by the system. Particularly, we looked into a way of compensating for poor behavior by lowering allocation of resources to such processes in subsequent intervals until control is restored. We found that our extension can bound the effect of the bad behavior over time.

We are looking into opportunities for generalizing our approach. Multiple coordinating actorgroup managers can be implemented to support distributed computation clusters. We also plan to add support for advance reservation of resources. Finally, we want to further strengthen our evaluation using case studies involving real applications.

**Acknowledgment.** This research was undertaken thanks in part to funding from the Canada First Research Excellence Fund.

# References

1. Agha, G.: ACTORS: A Model of Concurrent Computation in Distributed Systems. MIT Press, Cambridge (1986)
2. Jamali, N., Zhao, X.: Hierarchical resource usage coordination for large-scale multi-agent systems. In: Ishida, T., Gasser, L., Nakashima, H. (eds.) MMAS 2004. LNCS (LNAI), vol. 3446, pp. 40–54. Springer, Heidelberg (2005). https://doi.org/10.1007/11512073_4
3. The scala programming language (2017). http://www.scala-lang.org
4. Akka programming language (2017). http://www.akka.io
5. Zhao, X., Jamali, N.: Supporting deadline constrained distributed computations on grids. In: Proceedings of the 2011 ACM 12th International Conference on Grid Computing, ser. GRID 2011, pp. 165–172 (2011)
6. Jamali, N., Zhao, X.: A scalable approach to multi-agent resource acquisition and control. In: Proceedings of the International Conference on Autonomous Agents and Multiagent Systems, ser. AAMAS 2005, pp. 868–875 (2005)
7. Imam, S.M., Sarkar, V.: Selectors: Actors with multiple guarded mailboxes. In: Proceedings of the 4th International Workshop on Programming Based on Actors Agents, pp. 1–14 (2014)
8. Charousset, D., Hiesgen, R., Schmidt, T.C.: CAF - The c++ actor framework for scalable and resource-efficient applications. In: Proceedings of the 4th International Workshop on Programming Based on Actors Agents, ser. AGERE! 2014@SPLASH, pp. 15–28. ACM, New York (2014)

9. Decat, M., Bogaerts, J., Lagaisse, B., Joosen, W.: Amusa: middleware for efficient access control management of multi-tenant SaaS applications. In: Proceedings of the 30th Annual ACM Symposium on Applied Computing, ser. SAC 2015, pp. 2141–2148 (2015)
10. Li, Y., Deng, Y., Seet, R., Tang, X., Cai, W.: MASTER: multi-platform application streaming toolkits for elastic resources. In: Proceedings of the 23rd ACM International Conference on Multimedia, ser. MM 2015, pp. 805–806 (2015)
11. Boutin, E., et al.: Apollo: scalable and coordinated scheduling for cloud-scale computing. In: Proceedings of the 11th USENIX Symposium on Operating Systems Design and Implementation (OSDI), pp. 285–300 (2014)
12. Kamon: A tool for monitoring reactive applications (2017). http://kamon.io
13. Sematext SPM: A tool for performance monitoring (2017). https://sematext.com/spm
14. Google namespaces API (2017). https://cloud.google.com/appengine/docs/standard/java/multitenancy/
15. Karmani, R.K., Shali, A., Agha, G.: Actor frameworks for the JVM platform: a comparative analysis. In: Proceedings of the 7th International Conference on Principles and Practice of Programming in Java, ser. PPPJ 2009, pp. 11–20 (2009)

# Author Index

Printed in the United States
By Bookmasters